VGM Opportunities Series

OPPORTUNITIES IN
WORD PROCESSING CAREERS

Marianne Forrester Munday

Foreword by
Jerome Heitman
Executive Director
Professional Secretaries International

 **VGM Career Horizons**
a division of *NTC Publishing Group*
Lincolnwood, Illinois USA

Cover Photo Credits:

Front cover: upper left, Digital Equipment Corporation; upper right, Oakton Community College; lower left, NTC photo; lower right, DeVry Inc.

Back cover: upper left, Roosevelt University; upper right, Hewlett Packard; lower left and lower right, Oakton Community College.

Library of Congress Cataloging-in-Publication Data

Munday, Marianne Forrester.
   Opportunities in word processing careers / Marianne Forrester Munday.

      p.   cm.—(VGM opportunities series)
      Includes bibliographical references.
      ISBN 0-8442-8164-6 (hardbound) : $12.95. — ISBN 0-8442-8165-4 (softbound) : $9.95
      1. Word processing—Vocational guidance. I. Title. II. Series.
      HF5548.115.M86   1991
      652.5′023′73—dc20   90-50735
                                                     CIP

331.76s2
M9650

Published by VGM Career Horizons, a division of NTC Publishing Group.
©1991 by NTC Publishing Group, 4255 West Touhy Avenue,
Lincolnwood (Chicago), Illinois 60646-1975 U.S.A.

Manufactured in the United States of America.

1 2 3 4 5 6 7 8 9 VP 9 8 7 6 5 4 3 2 1

097861

ABOUT THE AUTHOR

Marianne Munday received her B.A. from Rutgers University and an M.B.A. from Virginia Polytechnic Institute and State University. She is presently director of community relations for a hospital in Hawaii. She is also a part-time business instructor.

Ms. Munday is also the author of *Opportunities in Crafts Careers,* published in 1987.

ACKNOWLEDGMENTS

The author would like to extend special thanks to the following individuals and organizations for their assistance in the preparation of this book:

Jim Munday, for his research, writing, and typing assistance
Bill Forrester, for his editorial assistance and numerous technical illustrations
Sharon Morrill, Natalie Urich, and Ronnie Stifter, who provided personal profiles
Marilyn Harris, El Camino Community College
Lee Soet, Kelly Services, Inc.
Keith Whelan, Little Company of Mary Hospital
Wang Laboratories
International Business Machines, Inc.
Lanier Business Products, Inc.
The International Association of Word Processing Specialists
Professional Secretaries International
Information Management and Processing Association
Office Technology Management Association
The Association of Information Systems Professionals
The Torrance, California Public Library Staff

v

To Jim

FOREWORD

Word processing has brought high-tech communications skills to the desktops of millions of office workers. It is an invaluable tool for businesses, enabling them to remain productive and efficient as they deal with the "information explosion" that is an inescapable part of modern life. The widespread use of automated office equipment allows secretaries and administrative assistants to increase the amount and complexity of their work. It allows the companies they work for to remain competitive.

Word processing enables the user to pass a document for review through electronic mail; it makes it possible to incorporate graphs and other images. Verification of spelling, on-line thesaurus capability, a readability index that indicates reading level—all are possible with modern word-processing equipment. Optical character recognition readers, which can scan a document and enter it into a computer, are being used in more and more offices. Voice recognition technologies, which allow the user to enter text into a computer just by speaking to the computer, may be the next innovation.

What do these high-tech advances mean for secretaries and other word processors? As individual word processors become more productive, will the number of openings in the field decline? Word processors may face stronger competition for jobs during the coming decade, but the volume of business transactions and the need to replace workers who transfer to other careers or leave the labor force, will guarantee a steady supply of jobs. The workers most likely to get those jobs will be those who are well educated and know a number of word-processing "languages."

Training for a word-processing career is available in many high schools, community colleges, and business schools. Many corporations and government agencies have continuing education courses to help their employees improve their skills and advance in their careers.

As you master word processing, you will find that you have developed a skill that allows you great flexibility. You may work part-time, take free-lance assignments, experiment with a home-based office, or choose a more traditional job setting. As a word processor, you will be making an important contribution to the productivity of American business while enjoying a challenging and professional career.

Jerome Heitman
Executive Director
Professional Secretaries International

INTRODUCTION

Without a doubt, we are living in the Computer Age. Computers play such an integral role in all of our lives that we often take them for granted. Banking, shopping, paying bills, even cooking: with the aid of computers, many of our routine personal transactions are carried out more quickly and efficiently than ever before.

Speed and efficiency are just two of many characteristics that have endeared computers to the business world. In offices around the globe, computers rapidly perform both mundane and complex tasks that were once done manually. Even the book you now hold was written with the aid of a computer, using an application known as word processing (or WP, for short). Word processing is a cost-effective application employed by many businesses wishing to improve their productivity. WP has only been around since the mid-1960s; still, the business world did not fully realize its wide range of uses until the 1970s.

Now, in the 1990s, WP has grown into a dynamic field that offers many interesting career opportunities in virtually every business category. Demand for skilled word processing equipment operators and other WP professionals is widespread. As a result, many women and men from diverse backgrounds, excited by the prospect of being at the forefront of this challenging field, are being attracted to the profession.

What exactly is word processing, and what role does it play in organizations? What kinds of career opportunities exist for WP professionals? What types of WP training are available, and how effective are they? What system(s) should a newcomer to the field take the time to learn?

The purpose of this book is to answer these questions and to provide the information you need to make an intelligent career decision. Whether you are just entering the job market or are considering making a career switch, you will find the kinds of information you need to decide if a position in the word processing field is really for you. If you are already employed in the word processing field, you will find helpful information on such topics as opportunities for advancement, spin-off careers, and continuing education.

Many experts predict that by the year 2000, word processing systems will replace the typewriter for most office uses. Given that scenario, a working knowledge of word processing will be essential for anyone who wishes to successfully compete in the business world. Therefore, regardless of your ultimate career decision, take some time to learn about this exciting technology.

CONTENTS

The automated office. Introduction to word processing. Origins of the field. The typewriter. Recent innovations.

Document production. A working definition of word
processing. Basic components of word processing
equipment. Types of word processors. Standard word
processing functions. User-friendly equipment. The
role of word processing in office operations. Advantages of word processing.

Word processing in the home. Organizational trends. Employment trends.

Determining your career goals. Becoming qualified. Investigating prospective employers. Preparing a resume and cover letter. Interviewing. After the interview. Choosing the right job. Continuing to plan your career.

CHAPTER 1

HISTORY AND DEVELOPMENT OF WORD PROCESSING

THE AUTOMATED OFFICE

The term office automation (OA) refers to the use of computers in office equipment to streamline operations. It is often said that we are in the midst of an office automation revolution. Technological innovations that improve the efficiency of office equipment and do away with many manual procedures are being introduced all the time. As a result, many businesses use a variety of sophisticated OA devices to increase their productivity.

The use of computers to streamline office procedures is not a new idea. As early as the 1940s, computerized (or electronic) machines capable of automatically storing, retrieving, and processing data were already in place and being used by some American businesses. These machines were called ''data processors'' because they were high-speed number crunchers capable of efficiently performing tasks such as payroll, accounting, and inventory control.

Today's data processing equipment is highly sophisticated, with the ability to compute huge and often complicated volumes of numerical data at rapid speeds. For most businesses, these computerized machines are standard tools that help them operate more efficiently, and therefore remain competitive.

Word processing, like data processing, is just one of many computer applications being utilized by businesses today. WP is a key aspect of office automation because it enables businesses to significantly improve their productivity. In a most basic sense, word processing entails giving computer capabilities to the office typewriter (although as you will see, WP is really much more than that). The result is faster, cheaper, and more effective written communications. For example, it has been estimated that the use of word processing systems can produce a 25–300 percent increase in the typewritten output of a typical secretary, and the cost savings to businesses can be just as impressive.

As more and more companies have weighed these benefits given the paperwork they produce and the cost of producing that paperwork, the demand for word processing systems has skyrocketed.

INTRODUCTION TO WORD PROCESSING

Word processing is often defined as "automated typing." That definition, however, is far from complete. Today, the term word processing is used to describe an entire system of streamlined work procedures, automated equipment, and skilled people.

At the heart of the WP system is the word processor, a very advanced version of the standard office typewriter. Although the word processor looks and acts a lot like a typewriter, it differs in a number of important ways. First, unlike the standard typewriter, the word processor has an internal memory that records and stores data (by means of disks, tapes, or cards) for later retrieval and use. Second, the word processor has sophisticated editing features that allow the user to easily add, delete, or move characters, words, or entire blocks of text. The word processor automatically rearranges the remaining text to a standard format. Third, most word processors have a video display screen, similar to a television screen, that enables the WP equipment operator to see what has been typed and how it will appear on the printed page *before* it is actually printed out. This feature is very important because it permits the WP operator to see mistakes and make corrections before printing a hard copy. Fourth, the word processor can automatically print out whatever has been recorded over and over again, allowing the WP operator to create any number of freshly typed "originals."

ORIGINS OF THE FIELD

It is not surprising that office technology has advanced to this level of sophistication. The human race has been trying to perfect the art of written communication for thousands of years. Primitive cave paintings, dating back to 20,000 B.C., have appropriately been described as "prewriting." They represent the first known attempts to communicate ideas without the aid of speech.

By 3,000 B.C., the Sumerians were using a much more advanced system of written communication. To improve record keeping, the Sumerian high priests began to inscribe business, legal, and historical information on clay tablets. Were these the rudiments of word processing? Probably so! Over time, the clay tablets that the Sumerians employed to record their writings were replaced by wood, papyrus, parchment, and eventually the high-quality paper that we use today. The stylus gave way to quills and finally to pen and ink.

Other advances that have had a significant impact on the evolution of written communications include the development of the Greco-Roman alphabet, which is still used today, and Johannes Gutenberg's invention of movable type in 1456, which made it possible to duplicate and mass produce written material.

THE TYPEWRITER

The invention that has had the greatest impact on office automation and word processing is the typewriter, which still ranks as the most widely used type of business machine in the world. The introduction of the typewriter virtually eliminated the need to hand-copy documents, which for centuries had been the only means of mass production. With the typewriter, high-quality written work could be produced at much faster speeds.

The Invention of the Manual Typewriter

Invention of the typewriter is generally attributed to Mr. Henry Mill, an English engineer. He received a patent for his invention in 1714. Little is known about his typewriter, however, because no description or model of it has ever been found.

Throughout the 1700s and 1800s, many inventors in both the United States and Europe tried to develop a more practical, efficient, and inexpensive version of Mill's machine. In 1867, Christopher Latham Sholes, with the assistance of Carlos Glidden and Samual W. Soule, invented the first successful manual typewriter. Sholes's machine consisted of understrike type bars that registered an impression of the typed characters beneath the typewriter roller. In essence, the individuals who operated these machines typed "blind." Because the typewriter keys hit the underside of the roller, it was impossible for the typist to see his or her work until it was finished. (In the early days, most typists were men. Also, the typists *themselves* were originally called "typewriters," and their machines were called "typographers.")

In 1874, E. Remington and Sons, the gun manufacturer, began to market the Sholes typewriter. Although the public was initially skeptical of the machine, Sholes's typewriter eventually revolutionized the business world. Soon, other companies began producing their own version of the typewriter. Even so, it would be several more years before the typewriter was truly accepted by the business community.

Improvements which aided in the typewriter's eventual acceptance included the invention of the shift key in 1878, which made possible the printing of both capital and small letters; complete visibility of writing in 1880; and the development of the tabulator in 1897, which allowed margins to be set. The first successful portable typewriter was marketed in the early 1900s. In the 1920s, one of the first true ancestors of office automation was invented—the *electric typewriter.*

Electric and Automatic Typewriters

Although Thomas Edison received a patent for an electric typewriter in 1872, it was not until the 1920s that a feasible model was introduced. It was powered by an electric motor and was much more efficient than manual machines. In 1935, International Business Machines Corporation (IBM) introduced the IBM Electromatic, a more streamlined model that greatly increased typing speeds and quickly gained wide acceptance in the business community.

During this same period, businesses began to express the need for a typewriter that would automatically produce individually typed copies of a form letter while retaining the appearance of the hand-typed original. The automatic, or repetitive, typewriter was developed in response to this need. This machine operated on the same principle as the player piano. Letters were code-punched onto a roll of paper tape. The perforations on the paper tape activated the typewriter keys, and could be used over and over again to produce repetitive copies of form letters.

Over the years, manufacturers offered many improvements to both the electric and automatic typewriters. During the 1960s, IBM led the field with a number of exciting innovations. In 1961, the company introduced the Selectric typewriter, an electric typewriter that operated without a movable carriage. Instead, the machine employed a removable typeball, or element, that contained all the letters and symbols found on standard typewriter keys. This revolving ball could print letters much faster that single-strike typewriter keys. The IBM Selectric was soon the most-used typewriter in the world.

IBM'S MT/ST—The First Text Editor

While the IBM Selectric was considered a major innovation, it only enabled typists to transfer words onto paper. Since it contained no corrections feature, text editing still had to be done using traditional methods—retyping, erasing, cutting and pasting. But those days were soon over.

In 1964, IBM combined the features of the Selectric with a magnetic tape drive and introduced the MT/ST, the Magnetic Tape/Selectric Typewriter. Heralded as the first electronic text-editing typewriter, the MT/ST changed the whole concept of typewriting. In fact, with the marketing of the MT/ST, the age of word processing had truly begun.

The MT/ST was a hard-wired machine. That is, all of the functions of the machine were coded on internal circuit boards. The MT/ST was attached to a console containing magnetic tape, as opposed to slower, nonerasable paper tape. With this combination, it was now possible to edit and revise documents. The magnetic tape stored text and allowed the typist to record over any errors. The tape could be used over and over again to produce flawless copies of documents. However, although the MT/ST was far superior to its predecessors, its editing capabilities were still greatly restricted by limited machine intelligence.

The term *word processing* has its roots in the development of the IBM MT/ST. Actually, "word processing" is the English translation of the German word, *textverarbeitung*. The term was coined in the late 1950s by Ulrich Steinhilper, a German engineer working for IBM. Steinhilper used the term to explain his theory that organizations could handle their written communications in a more systematic manner if their typing equipment was placed in a central location. There operators could type (or *process*) words without interruptions, which would save organizations both time and money.

In 1964, IBM again used the term to market the MT/ST as the world's first "word processing" machine.

RECENT INNOVATIONS

Following the invention of the MT/ST in the 1960s, the concept of word processing grew rapidly. Dozens of manufacturers joined the trend, producing increasingly sophisticated word processing equipment. One of the most exciting innovations was the introduction of microprocessors, or small computers, into the word processor. Microprocessors greatly expanded the machine's work capacity and allowed it to handle much more sophisticated text editing and formatting programs. The age of truly "intelligent" typewriters had arrived.

More recent innovations have included the addition of video display screens, which allow the user to see "soft" copies of his or her work. Magnetic disk storage devices; high-quality, high-speed printers; and sophisticated editing and formatting features are a few of the other advances. Many word processors now have the ability to communicate with each other, to transmit documents over phone lines, and to operate in both word processing and data processing modes.

Today, word processors are a standard part of many office systems, and are replacing the typewriter for many office uses. In the next several chapters, we will enter the world of word processing. Let's start by taking a more detailed look at what word processing is and what it can do.

CHAPTER 2

WORD PROCESSING BASICS

Whether or not you decide to pursue a career in the word processing field, take some time to become acquainted with this exciting technology. Word processing systems are already in place in most American businesses and a growing number of American homes. Now more than ever, a working knowledge of word processing is a valuable asset in both personal and professional life.

This chapter introduces a number of important word-processing concepts:

- Differences between the traditional document production cycle and the word processing document production cycle
- A working definition of word processing
- The basic components of word processing equipment
- General categories of word processing equipment
- Standard word processing functions
- The trend toward ''User-Friendly'' word-processing equipment
- The role of word processing in office operations
- The advantages of word processing

With this background, you will be well on your way to understanding what word processing is and how it is used by businesses, and you will be one step closer to making an informed career choice.

DOCUMENT PRODUCTION

The Traditional Cycle

Word processing systems still have not found their way into some business offices. In these offices, the standard electric typewriter is the key piece of equipment used by the secretary. All typed documents pass through the typewriter roller at least once, and often several times, on their way to final copy. Figure 2-1 depicts the traditional document production cycle.

Let's take a closer look at the steps in the cycle.

1. The author, or document originator, prepares a text to be typed by the secretary. The text is delivered to the secretary by means of dictation equipment, shorthand dictation, or longhand notes.

2. The secretary types the text using the office typewriter. As the secretary depresses the typewriter keys, the characters are immediately typed out on a piece of paper. The secretary reviews the completed text for typographical errors. If any are found, they are corrected by erasing, cutting and pasting, using white paint, or, in many instances, by completely retyping the document.

3. The text is returned to the document originator for approval.

4. The document originator proofreads the document and notes any corrections or revisions.

FIGURE 2-1
TRADITIONAL DOCUMENT PRODUCTION CYCLE

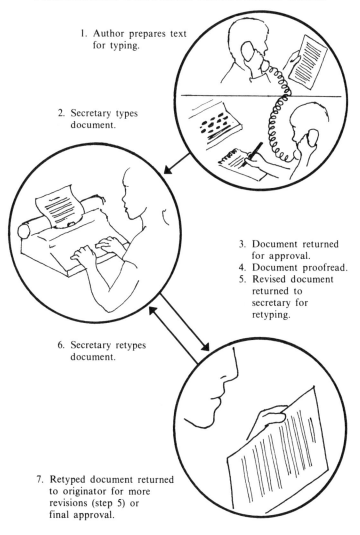

1. Author prepares text for typing.

2. Secretary types document.

3. Document returned for approval.
4. Document proofread.
5. Revised document returned to secretary for retyping.

6. Secretary retypes document.

7. Retyped document returned to originator for more revisions (step 5) or final approval.

5. If there are changes to be made, the document is returned to the secretary.
6. The secretary makes the necessary changes. This may require retyping all or large parts of the original document.
7. After all changes have been made, the revised document is returned to the document originator.

Steps 5 through 7 can be repeated as many times as necessary to produce a satisfactory final document.

As you can see, there are glaring inefficiencies in the traditional document production cycle. The secretary often spends an exorbitant amount of time making revisions to the original document. In many instances, the changes are so numerous that the entire document must be retyped. Because of these inefficiencies, secretarial productivity is much lower than it should be. In fact, it has been estimated that the secretary in this type of work environment spends only 20–25 percent of the day typing "new words."* The majority of the day is spent retyping and making corrections.

In addition, each time that all or part of a document is retyped, new typing errors are possible. Therefore, each new copy must be carefully and completely reviewed by the document originator or a qualified proofreader, a time-consuming and expensive effort.

The Word Processing Cycle

With the implementation of word processing systems, these types of inefficiencies can be minimized. Figure 2-2 shows the typical word processing document production cycle.

---

*Chambers, Harry. *Making the Most of Word Processing*. London: Business Books Ltd., 1982, p. 70.

FIGURE 2-2
WORD PROCESSING DOCUMENT PRODUCTION CYCLE

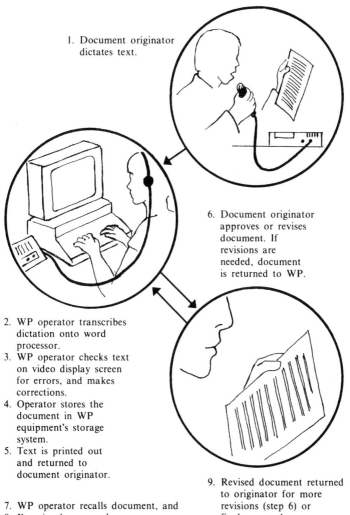

1. Document originator dictates text.

6. Document originator approves or revises document. If revisions are needed, document is returned to WP.

2. WP operator transcribes dictation onto word processor.
3. WP operator checks text on video display screen for errors, and makes corrections.
4. Operator stores the document in WP equipment's storage system.
5. Text is printed out and returned to document originator.

7. WP operator recalls document, and
8. Keys in changes *only.*

9. Revised document returned to originator for more revisions (step 6) or final approval.

Let's look at the steps in the cycle in more detail.

1. The document originator prepares a text for keying into the word processor. The text is delivered to the word processing equipment operator by means of dictation equipment, shorthand dictation, or longhand notes.

2. The WP operator transcribes or records the dictation onto the word processor. As the document is typed into the system by means of the WP keyboard, it immediately becomes visible on the video display screen. This allows the operator to see and correct any errors *before* the document is printed out. In fact, it should be stressed that a "hard copy" of the document is not made until the operator instructs the equipment to do so.

3. The WP operator checks the text on the video display screen for errors. If there are any, the operator types, or *keys,* the changes into the system, and the revisions immediately appear on the screen.

4. The WP operator stores the completed document on the WP equipment's storage system.

5. The text is printed out and returned to the document originator for approval.

6. If there are still changes or corrections to be made, the document is returned to the WP operator.

7. The original document is recalled from the word processor's memory and appears on the video display screen. The WP operator makes all changes to the original document by means of the machine keyboard. *Note: Only the changes need to be keyed in. The entire document does not have to be retyped.*

8. After all changes have been made, the revised document is printed out and returned to the document originator.

Steps 6 through 8 can be repeated as many times as necessary to produce a satisfactory final copy. Document revisions require very little operator time with word processing equipment. In fact, the word processing equipment operator spends an estimated 60–65 percent of the day typing new words.* The bottom line is that in most offices, document production improves considerably with the introduction of word processing systems.

A WORKING DEFINITION OF WORD PROCESSING

As our discussion of document production shows, word processing systems have a tremendous impact on office productivity. Word processing contributes to the production of written communications at faster speeds, lower costs, and with greater precision than methods used by most traditional offices. These are exciting claims and, as you will see, they are easily verified.

What exactly is word processing? Definitions range from simple to intricate. In fact, if you ask ten different people to define word processing, you will probably get ten different definitions. However, most office automation experts agree that the word processing concept encompasses much more than the WP equipment itself. The Association of Information Systems Professionals (AISP), profiled in Appendix B, defines word processing as:

> A system of trained personnel, specific procedures, and automated equipment that provides more efficient and economical business communications; usually involving the transformation of information into readable form.

---

*Chambers, Harry. *Making the Most of Word Processing*. London: Business Books Ltd., 1982, p. 70.

This definition will form the basis for our discussion of the word processing concept. We will be viewing word processing as a system composed of three integral parts: people, procedures, and equipment. Let's talk briefly about each.

The Word Processing Team

Successful word processing is a team effort. The word processing team is made up of a variety of trained professionals. Principals are individuals who originate documents for input into the WP system. We often refer to principals as authors or document originators. Principals must have a good working knowledge of their company's word processing procedures in order to use the system efficiently and effectively.

WP operators run the word processing equipment. They are responsible for keying, or typing, data into the word processor. WP operators work closely with principals and other WP personnel in the organization, including WP supervisors, managers, proofreaders, and trainers.

In addition, various support personnel help ensure the successful operation of the word processing system. Support personnel include equipment service technicians, trainers, systems analysts, salespeople, and many others.

Word Processing Procedures

When word processing is first introduced into the workplace, a set of standard procedures must be developed for efficient use of the system. These procedures describe how the word processing system is to be used by organization members and how work is to be completed by the WP staff.

In some businesses, centralized word processing centers, like those envisioned by IBM's Ulrich Steinhilper, are developed. These centers concentrate the WP equipment in a production environment where it can be used most efficiently. Other businesses find that a decentralized word processing structure better meets their document production needs. (See Chapter 3 for a detailed discussion of word processing organizational structures.)

Regardless of the organizational structure chosen, specific procedures regarding the origination and processing of documents must be developed and adhered to by all members of the organization. This ensures that document production is systematic and that the word processing system is being used to maximum advantage.

Word Processing Equipment

The word processor is the key piece of equipment in any WP system. Like the standard office typewriter, the word processor's primary function is to produce typewritten documents. Unlike the standard typewriter, however, the word processor has an internal memory that enables it to record and store information and later retrieve and manipulate that information.

Today, hundreds of word processing equipment models of varying levels of sophistication are on the market. While the systems may look different from one another, and may offer special features, they must perform five basic functions in order to be classified as word processors. Those functions are data entry, data storage, data retrieval, editing, and printing.

In order to better understand each of these five functions, let's take a closer look at the basic components of word processing equipment.

BASIC COMPONENTS OF WORD PROCESSING EQUIPMENT

Most word processors today have each of the following basic components: a keyboard, a video display terminal, an internal computer, an external storage system, and a printer. These components are pictured in Figure 2-3. Let's take a closer look at each.

The Keyboard. The keyboard is the place on the word processor where you enter data into the system. The WP keyboard is similar to that of a standard typewriter; it contains all the same keys, in the same order as on a typewriter. However, the word processing keyboard also has some additional keys, called command keys, that enable you to give the machine instructions, such as *delete, insert, move text, store, search,* and *print.* These additional keys can be found above or alongside the standard typing keys, as shown in Figure 2-4.

The Video Display Terminal (VDT). This device, also referred to as the cathode ray tube (CRT), is usually attached to the keyboard. It looks and operates much like a television screen. It allows you to see a ''soft copy'' of your text as it is typed into the WP system, before a hard copy is printed out.

As you type data into the word processing system by means of the keyboard, the corresponding characters immediately appear on the video display screen. Once they are visible, you can manipulate them by using your command keys. You can change characters, move them around, adjust them, or delete them. This is possible because you are working with electronic images as opposed to physical images composed of ink on paper.

Word processors vary in terms of the number of lines of data that their video screens are capable of displaying. In fact, some

FIGURE 2-3

**THE BASIC COMPONENTS OF
WORD PROCESSING EQUIPMENT**

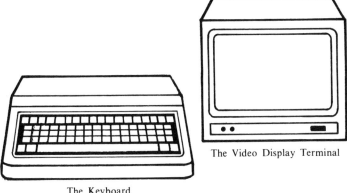

The Video Display Terminal

The Keyboard

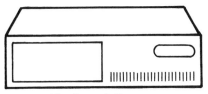

The Internal Computer

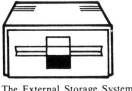

The External Storage System

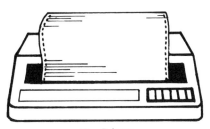

The Printer

FIGURE 2-4

WORD PROCESSOR KEYBOARDS

Command Keys Alongside
Standard Typing Keys

Command Keys Above
Standard Typing Keys

word processors do not have a VDT at all. Others display only one
or two lines of text. The majority of VDTs, however, show 24 or
more lines on the screen at one time.

A process called scrolling allows you to retrieve and see data
that is not currently displayed on the VDT. With the touch of a
button, you can move text up and down, or left and right, to view
and work with any portion of the text already entered into the WP
system.

The Internal Computer. Word processors are actually computer systems designed to perform WP functions. Therefore, they
have an internal computer composed of the microprocessor and
the internal memory.

The microprocessor is the central processing unit (CPU) in the
word processor. It is often called the word processor's ''brain.''

It is the internal part of the WP equipment that is responsible for processing, storing, and retrieving data from memory. The microprocessor performs all the mathematical and logical operations that keep the WP system running.

The other component of the internal computer is the memory. The word processor has two types of memory: ROM and RAM. ROM, or read only memory, is the equipment's permanent memory. It stores the machine's operating instructions which tell the CPU how to perform various functions.

Any text that you type into the word processing system goes into the RAM, or random access memory. This memory temporarily stores and handles all information that you give to the word processor, and can later be erased. It is important to remember that random access memory is temporary; it depends upon electric power. If the equipment loses power, the information in RAM is permanently lost. For this reason, WP operators routinely store their work on external storage devices, such as magnetic disks and tapes, for later use.

The External Storage System. The word processor's external storage system includes external storage devices, such as magnetic disks and tapes, and the storage media used to record the data on those devices.

External storage devices permanently record and store data keyed into the word processing system. Forms of external storage include magnetic disks, magnetic cards, magnetic tape, and paper tape. Today, magnetic disks are the most popular form of storage. The disks are flat, circular magnetic storage devices that are rotated like phonograph records by the system's disk drive.

Documents are stored on storage devices as "files." A file is defined as a "set of related information stored on a tape or disk." For example, while this book was being written with the aid of a word processor, each chapter was stored as a separate file on a magnetic disk.

External storage devices are important because they allow WP operators to permanently save their work. This eliminates the need to rekey text each time you want to work with it, and allows documents to be reprinted with greater speed and accuracy than possible with a standard typewriter.

In addition to magnetic tapes or disks, the external storage system includes the storage medium—the part of the word processor that actually holds the storage device. The storage medium records data on—or reads data from—the storage device. For example, a magnetic disk (storage device) is placed in a disk drive (storage medium). The disk drive reads data stored on the disk or writes new information onto the disk.

The Printer. The printer produces hard copies of your data. That is, it transforms your electronic data into ink on paper. Unlike the standard typewriter, the word processing printer is generally used only *after* the document is completed, rather than throughout the production process.

Printers can be classified as either impact or nonimpact. Impact printers transfer characters onto paper by means of an object striking an inked ribbon. Daisywheel printers and dot-matrix printers fall into this category. Nonimpact printers transfer characters onto paper without striking an object against the paper. Instead, characters are formed by heat, electrical charges, or ink jet (the spraying of ink onto paper). Laser printers are one type of nonimpact printer.

TYPES OF WORD PROCESSORS

The basic components of word processing equipment can be configured in a number of different ways. The four most common configurations, or categories, of word processing equipment are electronic typewriters, stand-alone word processors, shared logic systems, and distributed logic systems. If you are familiar with the specific characteristics of each equipment category, you will find it much easier to identify and evaluate alternative word processing systems.

Electronic Typewriters. Electronic typewriters, also known as low-level word processors or intelligent typewriters, are the most basic type of word processing equipment. They contain a microprocessor, limited memory, and some additional keys that make it possible to perform basic editing and formatting tasks.

Electronic typewriters have replaced standard typewriters at many secretarial workstations. These intelligent typewriters have some important advantages: they are relatively inexpensive, easy to learn and operate, and can perform simple text editing and formatting functions. On the negative side, limited memory capacity, inability to do complex editing, and single or double-line video displays (as opposed to full video display screens) make these machines inadequate for many business applications.

Stand-Alone Word Processors. These systems are the largest category of word processing equipment, and are so called because they are totally self-contained units. That is, they can function on their own without the assistance of another computer. There are two types of stand-alone word processors: blind stand-alone systems and stand-alone display systems.

Blind stand-alone systems consist of a keyboard/printer, internal computer, and a storage system. They do not have a video display screen.

Stand-alone display systems consist of all of the above plus a video display screen that allows the operator to see what is being typed before it is printed out. The printer is generally separate from the keyboard.

Shared Logic or Cluster Systems. These systems consist of several WP terminals that share the storage and processing power of one central computer. Unlike stand-alone systems, shared logic terminals are essentially "dumb." That is, they do not have their own internal computer, so they must be hooked up to a central computer in order to operate. These systems are often found in large offices where a number of word processing terminals can be linked to the central office computer, and, in some instances, to centralized disk drives and printers.

Shared logic systems represent a growing portion of the WP equipment market. A major advantage of these systems is that individual terminals can communicate with each other, which means that long typing jobs can be shared among several operators. One potential pitfall of shared logic systems is that all terminals rely on one central computer. If the central computer system malfunctions, all of the terminals become inoperative.

Distributed Logic Systems. These systems combine the best features of stand-alone and shared logic word processing systems. Like shared logic systems, distributed logic systems are made up of several WP terminals that share computer power, storage, and printers, and that can communicate with each other. However, unlike shared logic systems, individual terminals do have some intelligence of their own; they are capable of operating independently of the central computer.

STANDARD WORD PROCESSING FUNCTIONS

Word processors perform two basic kinds of functions: editing and formatting. Editing functions allow text to be keyed into the system and then revised. Formatting functions make it possible to alter the physical appearance of a document, such as width of margins, line lengths, and page lengths. This section describes some of the more common editing and formatting functions.

Editing Functions

Cursor Control. The cursor is a small character of light that shows you where the character you are about to type will appear on the video display screen. As you type text into the word processor, the cursor moves across the screen to show you where the next character you type will be located.

Once you have entered your text into the system, the cursor is also used to perform editing functions. Using the cursor control keys, the cursor can be moved up and down the screen, and left and right. By positioning the cursor at the point in the text where changes are to be made, you can manipulate (insert, delete, move) individual characters, words, or whole blocks of text.

Scrolling. Most video display screens only show about 24 lines of text at one time. Scrolling refers to the upward/downward or left/right movement of text lines so that another section of the text is visible on the screen. This feature makes it possible to view the entire document even though it is too lengthy to fit on the screen at one time.

Word Wrap. When typing on a standard typewriter, you must hit the return key when you reach the end of each line. The word wrap feature of word processing equipment eliminates this chore. Instead, the word processor automatically jumps to the next line when you reach the right margin. If a word is too long to fit at the end of a line, it is automatically moved down to the next line.

Insertion. The insertion feature allows you to add characters, words, phrases, paragraphs, and even pages in between other words or text. Insertions are made by moving the cursor to the position where you want to add something, giving the insertion command, if necessary, and then typing in the new text. The rest of your text automatically readjusts to make room for the new information.

Deletion. The deletion feature allows you to delete, or erase, characters, words, phrases, paragraphs, or even larger blocks of text. The surrounding text automatically readjusts itself.

Block Movements. In word processing, a block refers to any amount of text that you designate as a block—a word, sentence, paragraph, page or more. The block movement feature allows you to define a block of text by marking its beginning and end with the cursor. Once you have defined a block of text, you can manipulate the entire block at once; you can move it to another location in the text, delete it, or duplicate it.

Search. The search feature allows you to look for a word, or group of words, that appears in the body of your document. After your word processor has been told what word(s) to search for, it scans the text until it finds the words in question, and then displays them on the VDT.

Global Search and Replace. This feature allows you to search for a word, phrase, or sentence in your document and replace it with another. For example, suppose you discover that you have misspelled one word consistently throughout your document. The global search and replace function allows you to quickly search for each misspelling and to replace it with the correctly spelled word.

Spelling Verification. It is becoming more and more common for word processors to have their own internal dictionaries. The dictionary feature is used to check the spelling of each word in a document against the spelling in the dictionary. Misspelled words are highlighted on the VDT, and are corrected either by the operator or automatically by the word processor.

Formatting Functions

Setting Margins and Tabs. Before you begin keying in your document, you can set your right and left margins. The word processor is then programmed to type only within that space and will automatically move to the next line when you reach the right margin. It is also possible to set tabs at various locations on a line, just as you can with a standard typewriter.

Justification. On a standard typewriter, the left margin is always automatically aligned. The justification feature of the word processor allows you to have perfectly aligned left and right margins. In order to ''justify'' the right margin, the word processor inserts spaces of various sizes between words on each line so that all lines appear to be the same length.

Centering. This feature makes it possible to center a word, line, page, or even an entire document automatically. It is usually accomplished by inserting spaces at the beginning of a line. Centering is particularly useful when preparing charts because you no longer have to count characters and spaces as you do with a standard typewriter.

Hyphenation. With this feature, the word processor can automatically hyphenate a word that is too long to fit at the end of a line. The hyphenation feature is often used along with the justification feature to produce a perfectly aligned right margin.

Headings and Footings. Headings and footings are words or phrases that appear at the top and/or bottom of each printed page of your document. The automatic heading/footing feature lets you type the repetitive words only once and then have the word processor print them on every page. For example, when this book was being prepared for the publisher, the author's name had to appear at the top of each page of the manuscript. With a word processor, it only had to be typed once because the system was programmed to place the name as a heading on each page.

USER-FRIENDLY EQUIPMENT

The term "user-friendly" accurately describes much of the word processing equipment being marketed today. The designers of WP systems are constantly upgrading their products to make them more friendly toward you. This means that the equipment is getting easier to operate all the time. For example, many machines now understand commands that are in plain English (such as delete, insert, move) as opposed to "computerese."

In addition, it is not necessary to understand all of the internal intricacies of WP equipment in order to operate it. A basic knowledge of computer equipment and its capabilities will generally suffice. The more knowledgeable you are, however, the more marketable you will be.

THE ROLE OF WORD PROCESSING
IN OFFICE OPERATIONS

Every business has its own particular reasons for investing in a word processing system. In this section, we will look at some of the more common word-processing business applications. This list is not exhaustive, but is intended to make you aware of the variety of roles played by word processing systems in office operations.

Text-Editing. Most businesses turn out a variety of documents that go through a number of revisions before being finalized. Without a word processor, this can involve a seemingly endless cycle of typing, correcting, retyping, correcting, retyping. In the case of particularly long documents, the revisions process can be very tedious.

With a word processor, revisions can be made in a fraction of the time they would take on a standard typewriter. The WP operator calls the appropriate file up on the video display screen, keys in the required changes, and prints out the revised document. The result is faster turnaround time, which means greater productivity in the workplace.

Business documents that often require extensive text editing include proposals, manuscripts, long letters, handbooks, newsletters, project reports, promotional material, and technical manuals and reports, to name a few.

Repetitive Typing. Most businesses also have a number of form letters or standard letters that they use over and over again. The basic content of the letters remains the same; however, the headings, salutations, and certain key phrases in the letters may change. Before the introduction of word processing, form letters had to be typed out individually or, more frequently, photocopied with the variable information typed in separately. This was a tedious process, and invariably, the difference between the keyed-in text and the preprinted text was quite noticeable.

Word processing allows businesses to permanently store form letters so that they can be used frequently without having to be retyped. When needed, a document is simply recalled from memory and appears on the VDT. Variable data is then inserted within the body of the text as necessary. For example, if a company wants to send a mass mailing to its entire customer list, all it has to do is prepare one form letter; the word processor automatically inserts variable names and addresses. The time savings is tremendous, and the quality of each letter is perfect.

Many businesses also have standard paragraphs, or even larger amounts of information, that they use regularly in their documents or correspondence. With word processing, such boilerplate information can be stored and easily inserted into the body of otherwise original documents.

List Maintenance and Column Alignment. Every organization maintains lists of one sort or another. Among the more common are lists of customers, employees, files, indexes, inventories, parts, patents, phone numbers, products, and mailing addresses. Most of these lists need to be updated regularly. With a word processor, updates require very little time or effort. Merging stored mailing lists with form letters to quickly and economically produce mass mailings is one of the most cost-effective applications of word processing.

Tabular material—data that must be perfectly aligned in a document—is also easy to produce with a word processor. Financial reports, for example, often contain long, complex columns of figures. Word processing eliminates the difficulty associated with typing columns of data because of features such as automatic centering and automatic tabbing. Some word processors also have a function that automatically aligns decimal points.

Math Processing. Many word processors now contain mathematical support packages that are capable of performing calculations of numbers entered into the system. Some equipment is only capable of simple calculations, such as adding, subtracting, multiplying, and dividing. More sophisticated systems can perform a wide range of complex mathematical calculations.

ADVANTAGES OF WORD PROCESSING

What advantages do businesses derive from the use of word processing systems? Recent studies indicate that most businesses enjoy four major benefits from word processing and other automated systems: improved worker productivity; more accurate, higher-quality written work; faster turnaround time in document production; and reduced communications costs.

Improved Worker Productivity. Word processing allows businesses to properly utilize their most important resource—people. With word processing, document originators are able to use their time more efficiently and productively. Revisions can be made effortlessly; proofreading time is reduced dramatically, and, as a result, the quality and amount of written work produced increases. WP operators also become much more productive. Reports of increases in typewritten output range from 25 percent to over 300 percent.

More Accurate, Higher-Quality Work. Word processing results in the production of documents that are error-free and uniform in appearance. Editing techniques such as erasing, using white paint, and striking over mistakes are no longer necessary or acceptable.

Faster Turnaround Time. Because of the special editing and formatting features of WP equipment, operators can produce documents rapidly. Changes can be made quickly and typed out on high-speed printers. The result is faster turnaround time in the production of all typewritten communications.

Reduced Communications Costs. The cost of producing a typical one-page business letter on a standard office typewriter continues to skyrocket. Using a word processor, the same single-page letter can be produced for much less. When you consider the billions of letters that are produced by businesses each year, the cost savings associated with word processing can be enormous.

The bottom line is that effective use of word processing systems results in increased organizational efficiency and reduced communications costs. These benefits allow businesses to be more competitive and to more effectively meet their organizational goals.

CHAPTER 3

THE WORD PROCESSING ORGANIZATION

When word processing is added to the workplace, a number of internal organizational changes inevitably occur. In particular, new types of jobs for office workers are created. These new jobs often have a significant impact on the office structure, operating procedures, and career opportunities.

In this chapter, we will take a closer look at how businesses reorganize to accommodate word processing systems, and the kinds of career opportunities that result. First, however, let's look at the traditional office environment and how it can be affected by the implementation of word processing systems.

THE TRADITIONAL OFFICE STRUCTURE

In traditional offices, the secretary handles both administrative and typing tasks on a routine basis. In general, a one-to-one boss/secretary relationship exists. That is, each secretary performs all of the typing and nontyping tasks for one boss, as opposed to working for many individuals.

In this work environment, the secretary is expected to be a generalist, a jack(or jill)-of-all-trades. Responsibilities can include, but are not limited to, typing, taking dictation, proofreading, filing, handling mail, answering phones, and running errands. The amount of time spent on each of these activities will depend on the boss's work load and the nature of the business.

Obviously, this type of office arrangement can be very inefficient. For example, the secretary is often interrupted constantly by phone calls, visitors, and additional work requests from the boss while trying to type a "rush" document. At the other end of the spectrum, the traditional office structure can leave plenty of room for wasted time and boredom. In fact, it has been estimated that the average secretary spends about 15 percent of the day just waiting for work.

As office costs continue to increase, businesses must take a serious look at ways to cut expenses and increase productivity. Certainly, more efficient use of support staff, including secretaries, would do much to meet these goals. As we have seen, word processing systems go a long way toward improving worker productivity and controlling office costs.

THE WORD PROCESSING ORGANIZATION

We have defined word processing as a system of trained personnel, specific procedures, and automated equipment that provides more efficient and economical business communications. When businesses first implement WP, they often need to do some internal reorganization to accommodate the new system of personnel, procedures, and equipment.

Each business develops a unique word processing organizational structure to meet its own particular needs. As a result, WP structures are as many and varied as the businesses that develop them. In most cases, however, the organizational patterns that evolve fall into one of three general categories: centralized word processing, decentralized word processing, and word processing adapted to the traditional office structure.

Centralized Word Processing

In a totally centralized word processing organization, WP equipment is concentrated in a central location that serves multiple departments or groups within the organization. With centralization, general secretaries are replaced by two types of specialists: administrative specialists and correspondence specialists (whom we shall refer to as word processing specialists).

Administrative specialists perform all nontyping tasks for the organization, including file maintenance, phone work, scheduling appointments, researching data, and dealing with the public. In some organizations, they may also do a minimal amount of typing. Word processing specialists handle *all* office typing tasks, using word processing equipment. Both groups share the work of many executives, instead of being assigned to one boss. Such specialization of functions is thought to increase productivity and to offer more clearly defined career paths for both administrative and word processing personnel.

In most centralized WP organizations, separate word processing and administrative support (AS) centers are established, as shown in Figure 3-1. The word processing center performs all of the typing tasks for the organization. The administrative support center provides all other nontyping support.

With this type of office structure, document production procedures must be revised. Figure 3-2 shows the reorganized flow of written communications when separate WP and AS centers are

FIGURE 3-1

**ORGANIZATION OF SEPARATE WORD PROCESSING
AND ADMINISTRATIVE SUPPORT CENTERS**

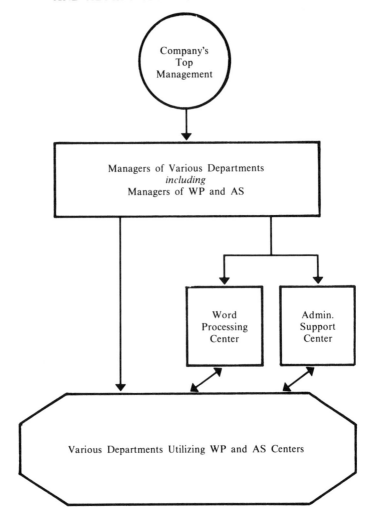

FIGURE 3-2

REORGANIZATION OF THE FLOW OF WRITTEN COMMUNICATIONS WHEN SEPARATE WP AND AS CENTERS ARE ESTABLISHED

ADMINISTRATIVE SECRETARY
in ADMINISTRATIVE SUPPORT CENTER (ASC)

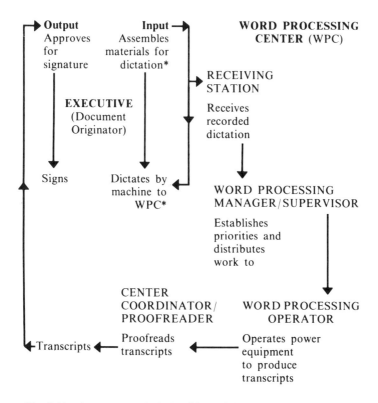

Output   **Input** →   **WORD PROCESSING**
Approves   Assembles   **CENTER** (WPC)
for   materials for
signature   dictation*

                                        RECEIVING
                                        STATION

EXECUTIVE   Receives
(Document   recorded
Originator)   dictation

Signs   Dictates by
                 machine to   WORD PROCESSING
                 WPC*   MANAGER / SUPERVISOR

                                        Establishes
                                        priorities and
                                        distributes
                                        work to

                 CENTER
                 COORDINATOR /   WORD PROCESSING
                 PROOFREADER   OPERATOR

                 Proofreads   Operates power
Transcripts   transcripts   equipment
                                        to produce
                                        transcripts

*The administrative secretary may also be the originator of dictation.

established. The new document production routine involves the following steps:

1. The administrative specialist in the administrative support center assembles materials for dictation.
2. The executive (or administrative specialist, in some instances) prepares the document using dictation equipment.
3. The dictation is received at the word processing center.
4. The word processing supervisor establishes priorities and assigns the work to one or more word processing operators.
5. The word processing operator types the document into the word processing system. A hard copy is printed.
6. The document is proofread by a member of the word processing staff.
7. The document is sent back to the administrative specialist for preliminary approval.
8. After all necessary corrections have been made, final approval and sign-off are given by the executive.

In order for the system to work effectively, these standard operating procedures must be consistently followed by all members of the office staff.

Figure 3-3 shows a typical organizational plan for the word processing center in a large company. This company has both day and night word processing shifts to ensure maximum use of the equipment. The WP center is staffed by a variety of word processing specialists, including trainees, operators, proofreaders, trainers, schedulers, a supervisor, and a manager.

Decentralized Word Processing

In a decentralized word processing organization, smaller clusters of word processing equipment take the place of large, central-

FIGURE 3-3

**ORGANIZATION PLAN FOR A
WORD PROCESSING CENTER**

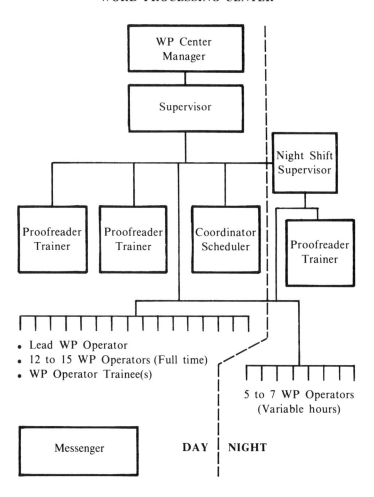

ized WP pools. For example, a company may establish separate WP centers for each department or floor of the organization.

In a decentralized environment, administrative tasks may be performed by smaller administrative support centers, individual secretaries, or a combination of the two.

Word Processing Adapted to the Traditional Office

A growing number of businesses are choosing to adapt their word processing systems to the traditional office structure (one boss/one secretary). The widespread availability of low cost, multifunctional business computers has made it possible to locate equipment at individual secretarial workstations. The secretary in this environment handles both administrative and word processing functions.

WORD PROCESSING POSITIONS

Word processing has created new job opportunities for office workers who develop word processing and/or administrative skills. What jobs are available within a word processing organization? Just as there is no standard organizational plan for word processing organizations, there are no standard word processing job titles. This section will introduce you to common word processing positions. Chapters 4, 5, and 6 provide more detailed information on qualifications, training, and employment opportunities.

Word Processing Trainee

The word processing trainee generally has 0–12 months of word processing experience. The position requires typing proficiency (45 to 80+ words-per-minute), English grammar skills, and the ability to understand and work with sophisticated electronic machinery. The trainee learns to use the word processor to do simple correspondence jobs, such as recording routine transcription and playing out prerecorded documents. The trainee may also be responsible for logging production time and volume, and for some proofreading.

Word Processing Operator

The word processing operator, often called a word processing specialist, generally has a minimum of six months of word processing experience. In addition to carrying out all of the duties of the trainee, the word processing operator handles lengthier, more complex projects, revises documents as necessary; has learned more advanced equipment and skills; and assists other operators as needed. Familiarity with company terminology and document production procedures is necessary.

Some companies with large word processing centers have various levels of word processing operators. The Association of Information Systems Professionals lists word processing operator, specialist I, and specialist II as three common classifications.

Word Processing Supervisor

The word processing supervisor generally has a minimum of two years of word processing experience and is a highly proficient WP operator. The supervisor is responsible for the day-to-day operation of the word processing center. This entails scheduling and coordinating the work, maintaining quality control, providing information to the rest of the company regarding the status of documents and workload, and identifying areas in the department for potential improvement. Some supervisors may also have some responsibility for budgets and equipment recommendations.

In larger companies, the word processing supervisor reports to the word processing manager.

Word Processing Manager

The word processing manager directs and controls the entire word processing operation. This involves developing procedures for word processing operations; selecting, directing, and guiding WP personnel; maintaining liaison with upper-level management; and designing word processing systems. In addition, the manager is responsible for the word processing budget, production reports, training schedules, and the coordination of activities within the administrative side of the organization.

Proofreader

The proofreader checks typed documents for spelling, grammar, and typographical errors. The job also entails keeping up-to-date on any special jargon or technical terms used by the organization. Proficiency in use of the English language and a keen eye for detail are essential.

Word Processing Trainer

The word processing trainer usually has a minimum of 24 months of word processing experience and is responsible for teaching new operators and others in the organization how to use the word processing system. The trainer may also instruct document originators about the use of dictation equipment and other procedures that help to ensure efficient use of the word processing system. The position requires superior equipment knowledge, an interest in teaching, and excellent communication skills.

Administrative Specialist

The administrative specialist generally assists two or more executives with day-to-day administrative details. The position involves little or no typing, but includes administrative support duties such as maintaining files, scheduling appointments, answering and making telephone calls, dealing with the public, and sometimes composing business communications. More specialized support can include research, mathematical calculations, proofreading, and editing.

The position requires organizational skills, tact and diplomacy, and the ability to communicate with individuals at all levels of the organization. At a minimum, a high school education is required. College-level business courses are highly recommended.

CHAPTER 4

IS A WORD PROCESSING CAREER FOR YOU?

Is a word processing career really for you? Before making such an important decision, take some time to assess your individual interests, skills, and personality traits to see if they are compatible with a word processing career. This chapter provides the following information to help you make that assessment:

- Characteristics of the field
- Employment outlook
- Qualifications for word processing personnel
- What word processing operators like/dislike about their jobs
- How secretaries feel about word processing
- Working conditions
- Salaries
- Why you should learn word processing

WORD PROCESSING: A DYNAMIC, EXPANDING FIELD

If you are interested in a career in an expanding industry, you should carefully consider word processing. It is still a relatively young field that is growing. Sales of word processing systems are booming. This translates into hundreds of thousands of word processing systems in the workplace, ranging from electronic typewriters to highly sophisticated word/information processors.

Why are businesses investing so heavily in word processing systems? In recent years, office costs have skyrocketed while worker productivity has remained relatively constant. In addition, there has been a paperwork explosion in the workplace because of the ever increasing need for more and better information. In order to remain competitive in such an environment, businesses have had to look for ways to increase worker output and reduce costs.

Word processing provides these results. As we have seen, word processing helps to control office costs, improves worker productivity, and makes it possible to disseminate information quickly and accurately.

Given these advantages, it is not surprising that most businesses have already invested in some type of word processing system, or plan to do so in the near future. The result is a demand for word processing personnel who can maintain and operate those systems.

EMPLOYMENT OUTLOOK

The United States Department of Labor, Bureau of Labor Statistics reports that the demand for word processors is expected to decline through the year 2000, despite the increasing volume of business transactions and correspondence. Ironically, this decline is a reflection of the increased worker productivity made possible by word processors. Technological advances in word processing allow fewer workers to handle a larger amount of work. In addition, personal computers are becoming more popular, encouraging some executives to do keyboarding themselves rather than delegating all assignments to word processing personnel.

Despite these changes, there will be a continuing need for word processors to replace those who move on to other occupations or leave the workplace. This need is expected to create many thousands of word processing jobs each year. Strong technical skills and knowledge of more than one word processing "language" will increase your opportunities for employment in the field.

Although an estimated 95 percent of word processing positions are filled by women, men are increasingly being drawn to the profession. Word processing offers both men and women an opportunity to be at the forefront of office automation. In addition, they find that a word processing background can be a stepping stone to a wide variety of career options. Experienced word processing operators often go on to supervisory positions and other information processing careers.

QUALIFICATIONS FOR WORD PROCESSING PERSONNEL

As we have discussed, any successful word processing system includes professional people, WP equipment, and standard procedures. While all three elements are essential, it is professional people who keep the word processing systems up and running efficiently. Without highly skilled personnel, word processing systems would be little more than masses of machinery.

Employers know that the selection of a good word processing operator can greatly improve office productivity and the quality of written work. On the other hand, the selection of a poorly trained operator can have disastrous effects on productivity, work quality, and office morale. Therefore, employers are very concerned about getting the best people to operate their word processing systems.

There are two categories of characteristics that employers look for in their word processing personnel: technical skills and personal traits. Technical skills include those office, language, and math skills that are necessary to be successful in the word processing field. Personal traits are those individual qualities that employers look for in a word processing professional. Take some time to review these characteristics and determine whether or not they describe you. Please note that although the following discussion centers on the WP operator, these technical skills and personal traits are important for any position in word processing.

Technical Skills

Typing Skills. Aspiring word processing operators should be able to type quickly and accurately. Standards for entry-level word processing positions range from 45 to 80 + words-per-minute, depending on the nature of the work. Some employers stress typing skills first and equipment knowledge second. Others are more concerned that you are able to operate their particular brand of equipment, and believe that typing speed comes with experience on the equipment.

An Interest in Machines. The ability to understand and work with modern, technical equipment is essential. Although most word processors are user friendly, they are, without a doubt, more intricate than standard typewriters. You should enjoy the challenge of working with computerized equipment and be willing to do so on a daily basis.

English Language Skills. A strong command of the English language, including knowledge of English grammar and usage, is also imperative. Word processing operators should be able to produce documents that are free of grammar, spelling, and punctuation errors. In some instances, editing skills may be required.

The Ability to Read, Follow, and Interpret Directions. Word processing operators should be able to read and interpret documents without constant supervision. Of course, questions should be asked whenever you are unable to interpret the document originator's work, but common sense should be used whenever possible.

Personal Traits

Professionalism. Professional word processing operators are resourceful, independent, and willing to take initiative. Professionalism also implies loyalty to your boss and enthusiasm about your work.

An Interest in Word Processing. Operators should enjoy typing and working with modern equipment. This interest should translate into neat, accurate work in which both the employer and operator can take pride.

Dependability. A commitment to reporting to work as scheduled and on time is essential to efficient word processing operations. Absenteeism and tardiness create backlogs and place unnecessary pressure on both the employer and coworkers.

Ability to Handle Pressure. Operators must regularly cope with difficult assignments, deadlines, and changing priorities.

Pressures and frustrations are common in such an environment. However, WP operators must be able to handle these pressures with a positive attitude and patience.

Concentration. Operators must sit at their word processing terminals for long periods of time. In fact, many operators spend 80 percent or more of the day at their equipment. The ability to concentrate and remain confined to one area is essential.

Human-Relations Skills. WP operators must be "team players." They must be able to work well with principals, technicians, secretaries, and other members of the word processing team. A cooperative, helpful attitude can have a big impact on productivity and office morale.

Task-Orientation. The primary job of the word processing operator is to produce printed materials accurately and efficiently. Output is closely scrutinized, and the quantity and quality of that output can be easily measured and evaluated. WP operators must be able to perform well in this type of production environment.

Employers are always assessing the qualifications of their word processing personnel, as well as their other employees. Because personal traits are not easily evaluated, employers must make subjective appraisals of these characteristics. Technical skills, on the other hand, are much more easily measured. A variety of production-oriented techniques exist and are currently used by employers as skill evaluations. These techniques include line and page counts (to see how many lines or pages of text an operator produces in a particular period of time), turnaround time in producing documents, and error rates. As a WP operator, you should be ready to have your work scrutinized in this manner.

WHAT WORD PROCESSING OPERATORS
LIKE/DISLIKE ABOUT THEIR JOBS

A number of recent studies have explored how word processing operators feel about their jobs. What are some of the positive and negative aspects of their positions? A summary of that information follows.

Positive Aspects of Word Processing Positions

Most word processing operators agree that their positions offer the following:

1. An opportunity to learn and use sophisticated office equipment. WP operators are at the forefront of office automation. They develop technical skills that can be adapted to a variety of office equipment, including word processors, data processors, and multifunctional business computers.
2. The ability to produce higher volumes of work in less time than traditional typists. Substantial increases in productivity are reported by most word processing operators. Such immediate results make their jobs more rewarding and less stressful, and free them to take on more challenging tasks.
3. Additional career opportunities because of word processing skills. With the right amount of training and experience, WP operators can go on to positions as WP supervisors, managers, and trainers. They can also use their word processing expertise to branch out into new careers in fields such as sales, computer programming, and teaching. They are often able to arrange flexible work schedules or assignments with temporary employment agencies.
4. An opportunity to work with a variety of professionals. WP operators work closely with principals and other WP pro-

fessionals in the organization. They also come in contact with manufacturers' representatives.

5. A variety of work, which keeps them busy and interested. Because word processing makes operators more efficient and able to produce a higher volume of work, they often have time to take on a greater variety of work involving more challenge and responsibility.

Negative Aspects of Word Processing Positions

Word processing operators do have some complaints about their jobs. These include the following problems:

1. Potential health hazards associated with using word processing equipment. Complaints range from musculoskeletal strain, headaches, backaches, and eyestrain to fatigue and stress-related illnesses.

2. Excessive stress and job pressures. Some operators report that principals and WP supervisors have unrealistic expectations of the capabilities of the WP equipment. They therefore place unreasonable demands on operators, making their jobs stressful.

3. Being treated like a machine instead of a person. This is one of the biggest complaints of word processing operators. The intensive production orientation of some companies can translate into a lack of concern for the personal needs of WP operators. This lack of concern can result in poor motivation, emotional and physical stress, and frustration among equipment operators.

4. Poor training on word processing equipment. Training programs offered by employers and schools vary considerably. In some instances, the training is inadequate, and operators are less productive as a result.

5. Lack of appreciation by supervisors and others. Some WP operators feel that their capabilities are unrecognized. They want to be told when they perform well and to be treated with respect and consideration.
6. Unfair work measurement techniques. Some word processing organizations closely measure and evaluate each operator's output and performance. Because the degree of difficulty varies from one assignment to the next, it can be unfair to use techniques such as line and page counts to compare and evaluate operators.

Certainly, the degree to which any of these problems exists varies greatly from one employer to the next. However, when evaluating any employer, try to determine if any of these problems is a potential concern. Spend some time talking with other members of the word processing staff. In most instances, they will be your most reliable source of information about working conditions at the company.

HOW SECRETARIES FEEL ABOUT WORD PROCESSING

The introduction of word processing to an organization inevitably has a considerable impact on all of its employees. The secretarial staff, in particular, feels the impact, because they are frequently the ones who will be trained to operate the new equipment. Many companies report that the introduction of word processing initially produces a lot of apprehension among members of the secretarial staff. Fear of computers, anxieties about job security, and skepticism about the equipment's capabilities appear to be the major concerns.

Studies indicate that, fortunately, this apprehension dissipates over time. With training and experience, most secretaries develop a very positive attitude toward word processing. In fact, most secretaries believe that office automation has "beneficial effects on the secretarial profession, permitting them to be more efficient and produce a higher volume of work. This, in turn,...allow[s] them more time to take on tasks involving greater challenge and responsibility...."* Secretaries also believe that office automation opens up new career opportunities for them, including managerial and administrative positions and more specialized positions in data processing and office automation.

These findings are very heartening. They suggest that word processing is a field that offers challenge, opportunities, and potential for growth for members of the secretarial profession.

WORKING CONDITIONS

Today, manufacturers and employers alike are making every effort to provide a safe, comfortable work environment for word processing employees. The fact remains, however, that most word processing operators sit at a terminal for at least 80 percent of their work day. This has led to a number of health-related operator complaints.

Potential Health Problems

VDT-Related Problems. Recent studies have linked video display terminals to eyestrain, migraine headaches, nausea, lower

---

*"How Secretaries Relate to the Age of Information," *The Office,* May 1983, pp. 112–113.

and upper back pain, other musculoskeletal problems, and increased levels of job stress.

Job Stress. Quotas, difficult assignments, deadlines, and changing priorities can all take their toll on the WP operator. High levels of job stress can potentially lead to stress-related illnesses, including coronary heart disease.

Sitting for Long Periods of Time. Excessive sitting combined with poorly designed chairs can lead to backache and can also aggravate hemorrhoids, varicose veins, and other circulatory conditions.

Fatigue. Intense concentration can lead to both muscular and mental fatigue.

Noise. High levels of machine noise can be annoying and potentially harmful to hearing.

The Solution: Ergonomics

Ergonomics is the application of biological and engineering data to problems pertaining to people and machines. In response to worker complaints about health problems related to their word processing positions, WP equipment and furniture manufacturers are including ergonomic features in word processing workstations.

Ergonomic furniture has been designed to provide WP operators with more comfortable working conditions. There are now special chairs with adequate support and work surfaces that are the correct height. In addition, video display screens that are flicker free and can be adjusted for brightness are becoming standard. Some companies have had their VDT screens fitted with special filters designed to reduce glare. Adequate consideration is also being given to overhead lighting to minimize eyestrain. Printers are getting less noisy all the time, and most employers now make every effort to station noisy printers away from the word processing work areas.

Employers have a responsibility to provide a suitable work setting for their employees. When evaluating a potential employer, consider the following:

- What types of word processing furniture are used? Do chairs give sufficient support to operators? Are desks the proper height and spacious enough to support work requirements? Can equipment height be adjusted?
- Are WP video display screens flicker free? Is there proper overhead lighting?
- Are noise levels acceptable?
- Is an adequate number of breaks allowed? The National Institute for Occupational Safety and Health (NIOSH) recommends a 15-minute break every hour for individuals under high visual demands.
- Is the general environment favorable?

If you are satisfied with your answers to these questions, you may be on your way to a pleasant, new working relationship.

SALARIES

The word processing field offers attractive salaries. Certainly, your salary will be affected by the industry you choose, the company you work for, the region of the country you live in, and your experience and ability. On the average, however, you will

Average Weekly Earnings in 12 Metropolitan Areas, 1988

Metropolitan Area	Average Weekly Earnings
Austin, TX	$291–$335
Baltimore, MD	$324–$370
Boston, MA	$332–$416
Chicago, IL	$340–$392
Cincinnati, OH	$315–$330
Cleveland, OH	$291–$365
Hartford, CT	$313–$356
Nassau County, NY	$309–$344
Orlando, FL	$295–$357
Phoenix, AZ	$293–$348
San Antonio, TX	N/A $318
Tampa, FL	$233 N/A

Source: Bureau of Labor Statistics, Area Wage Surveys, 1988

find that word processing positions offer higher salaries than those found in more traditional office positions.

The figures above represent average weekly salaries for word processing operators. They are provided to give you an idea of the range of salaries that are potentially available to you. Remember, though, that these figures are just averages. Many factors can influence the particular salary that you will be offered.

Word processing salaries continue to increase at a faster pace than salaries for more traditional office positions. One of the best ways to keep up-to-date on word processing salary trends is to regularly review salary surveys. The Association of Information Systems Professionals (AISP) prepares an annual WP salary study that can be obtained by writing to them at 104 Wilmot Road, Suite 201, Deerfield, IL 60015. The AISP study provides a summary of salary data for the entire United States, and by region and industry. In addition, an annual salary survey is produced by

Infosystems, a monthly magazine available in most libraries. The survey, published in the magazine's June issue, provides average weekly salaries for word processing positions nationwide.

You can also get a better idea of the salary you can command by reading help-wanted ads in your local newspaper, talking with potential employers about the salaries they offer, talking with employment counselors/recruiters about your worth in the WP job market, and talking to people already employed in your field of interest.

Of course, the more specialized training and experience you have, the more likely you are to surpass the WP salary averages.

WHY YOU SHOULD LEARN WORD PROCESSING

Whether or not you decide to enter the field, a working knowledge of word processing can be a long-term asset. On a personal level, the ability to use word processing equipment can save you considerable time when it comes to writing reports, keeping personal records, and even shopping and paying bills. It has been estimated that in the not-too-distant future, most homes will have some type of word processing equipment.

Professionally, word processing expertise can be a real advantage. As businesses become more computer-oriented, most positions will require some familiarity with this technology. You will be at the leading edge of the office automation revolution if you have a working knowledge of word processing equipment.

CHAPTER 5

TRAINING FOR A WORD
PROCESSING CAREER

Typist Wanted: High School Graduate, 55 + words per minute

Not so long ago, help-wanted advertisements like this one dominated the employment sections of newspapers. Typists were in great demand because they were responsible for the production of most written communications in the workplace.

Training for a position as a typist was a relatively simple and straightforward process. Typewriters did not differ from one another very much. Therefore, it was possible to learn to type on equipment at virtually any high school, community college, secretarial or business school, or even at home, and easily transfer those skills to the workplace.

For proficient typists, employment opportunities abounded in practically every business category. And employers could easily determine proficiency. For example, if a 60 + words-per-minute typist was needed, the employer could sit applicants down at a standard office typewriter and test their skills.

Because of the proliferation of automated office equipment, the heyday of the conventional office typist who can only operate a standard typewriter is over. In fact, some job analysts have gone so far as to describe the conventional typist as an "endangered species."

In the present job market, word processing expertise is quickly becoming a prerequisite for many office positions. Today, high school graduates with typing ability often need to acquire an additional, more technical skill such as word processing just to land an entry-level job.

Mastering the fundamentals of word processing is without a doubt more difficult than learning basic typing skills. As we have seen, the capabilities of word processing equipment are far greater than those of a standard typewriter. Because there are so many word processing functions to be understood and mastered, it takes three to six months, typically, for a WP operator to become proficient on the equipment. Basic typing skills can often be learned in as many weeks.

Even before an aspiring WP operator begins to train, there are numerous important decisions he or she has to make. With so many different word processing equipment models to choose from, which system or systems should you take the time to learn? Having made that decision, where should you obtain your training? What constitutes good training?

These are all very important questions. Yet, there is no single correct answer to any of them. The purpose of this chapter is to provide you with the kinds of information you need in order to choose the training that is most appropriate for you.

DECIDING WHICH SYSTEM(S) TO LEARN

Which word processing equipment should you learn? This is a very important decision because it will undoubtedly influence the kinds of jobs you will be qualified to perform. Some employers are only willing to hire WP operators who have been trained on their particular brand of equipment.

There are just too many systems currently on the market to be knowledgeable about each one. Therefore, you will want to learn the WP system that best matches your individual interests and needs. The following guidelines should assist you in making an informed decision:

- Familiarize yourself with the major components of word processing equipment, general categories of equipment, and basic word processing functions, as outlined in Chapter 2. With this background, you should be able to knowledgeably compare alternative systems and weed out those that are incompatible with your needs.
- Study the job market that is of interest to you. You will find that different industries prefer different types of equipment. You can determine the system that best matches your career objectives by talking to WP employment counselors, scrutinizing help-wanted advertisements (many ads now list the specific word processors that operators will be working on), talking to the personnel offices of companies you are interested in working for, and talking to WP operators currently employed in your field of interest.

EVALUATING TRAINING PROGRAMS

Although there are a variety of options to choose from, there is no single best way to obtain word processing training. Each type of training has potential advantages and disadvantages. Therefore, you should carefully consider each option available to you and pick the one that best suits your circumstances.

When evaluating your alternatives, consider the following:

WP Equipment. The facility you choose should train on state-of-the-art equipment that is being used in the job market that is of interest to you. Make sure that there are enough machines to accommodate class size, and that you are given plenty of opportunity to practice on the equipment.

Teaching Philosophy. Ideally, your program should include a combination of conceptual and operational training. Conceptual courses teach the fundamentals of word processing—what it is, what its capabilities are, how it can be used to maximum advantage. Operational training teaches students how to operate the WP equipment.

Training Environment. Word processing is taught in a variety of settings: formal classroom instruction, one-on-one instruction, and informal group instruction. You should choose the training environment that makes you feel comfortable. Do not settle for overcrowded classrooms, cramped work spaces, or an impersonal approach to teaching.

Course Length. Length of WP training can range from as little as two weeks to two or more years. The amount of WP education that you decide on should reflect the amount of time you have available and your long-term career goals. In all cases, evaluate course length to determine if there is adequate training time to meet your individual needs.

Job Placement and Internships. Formal job placement programs and internship programs associated with training programs are becoming more and more common. If possible, choose a program that offers those added advantages.

TYPES OF TRAINING AVAILABLE

Once you have clarified your personal objectives, you are ready to learn word processing. Several common avenues of training are available to you:

College-level training
Company-sponsored training
Word processing equipment vendor training
Business and secretarial school training
Training through temporary help services
Training by independent consultants
Self-instruction

Unfortunately, there is no comprehensive listing of training sources. Consult your phone book, the local library, and career guidance counselors for help in gathering this information. In addition, the professional associations listed in Appendix B may be able to provide some assistance.

Let's take a closer look at some of the more popular training alternatives.

College-Level Training

Today, many word processing/information processing management positions require an advanced education. If you are looking to move on to the management ranks, you will want a well-rounded educational background. Therefore, you should consider attending college.

Most community colleges and a growing number of four-year colleges now offer some amount of word processing training. Some schools offer a few word processing courses; others have developed entire word processing programs. There are word processing certificate programs that average one year in length. There are also two-year associate degree programs that include a larger number of academic and word processing courses. Today, a four-year degree program, especially in business administration or business education, can also include word processing courses in its curriculum.

The following curricula are provided to give you a sampling of the types of courses you might expect to take at the community college level.

A TYPICAL CERTIFICATE PROGRAM (ONE-YEAR)

The student earns a word processing certificate upon successful completion of 30 semester units of courses (24 units of required courses; 6 units of electives).

First Semester

Course	Units
Effective English for Business	3
Records/Information Management	2
Office Automation Concepts	2
Machine Transcription	2
Electronic Typewriting	1
Introduction to Business*	3
Career Orientation*	2
	15

Second Semester

Course	Units
Written Business Communications	3
Office Procedures	3
Word Processing Management	1
Expert Typewriting**	3
Word Processing on a Dual Display System	
or	
Word Processing on a Shared Logic System	4
Microcomputer Word Processing Applications	1
	15

*Electives
**Beginning and Advanced Typing (six units) are prerequisites.

A TYPICAL ASSOCIATE DEGREE PROGRAM (TWO-YEAR)

The student earns an Associate in Arts degree with a word processing major upon successful completion of 60 semester units. This includes 30 semester units of courses similar to those earned in the WP certificate program. The student must also complete 30 additional semester units, to include general education requirements and electives.

General Education Requirements

Course	Units
Natural Sciences	3
Social & Behavioral Sciences	3
Humanities	3
English Composition	3
Communication & Analytical Thinking	3
Contemporary Health	3
Mathematics	3
Electives	9
	30

The cost of attending college can be high. Many four-year programs at private schools run several thousand dollars per year. Community colleges and state colleges and universities are usually less expensive. If you do enough research, you should be able to find a program, full-time or part-time, that matches your budget and circumstances.

TIPS ON CHOOSING A COLLEGE

- Determine the length of time and amount of money you have available to spend on your education. This will help you decide whether to look at community colleges or four-year programs.
- Contact the admissions offices of the schools that you are interested in to be sure that they offer word processing training. Ask for a catalog of courses and also ask to be put in contact with the department that offers word processing. They can provide you with more detailed information about their word processing program.
- Make sure that the word processing equipment being used is up-to-date and that word processing courses are well-rounded.
- Talk with students currently enrolled in the programs to determine if they are satisfied with their training.
- Evaluate job placement services and internship possibilities.
- Find out if you can enroll as a special student and take only one or two word processing courses or if you must complete enrollment as a regular full-time student. You might want to start school on a part-time basis to evaluate the program and determine your interest in word processing.

The Association of Information Systems Professionals provides a list, by state, of colleges offering information/word processing education. It can be obtained by writing to the Association at the address listed in Appendix B. Since the list is not complete in every area, you should contact local schools to find out if they offer word processing training.

If you are currently employed, find out if your employer will pay for you to take word processing courses. Many do. You might be able to start your college education on a part-time basis without having to leave your present job.

Company-Sponsored Training

If you are presently employed by a company that uses word processing equipment and you are interested in learning the system, you are probably in luck. Many companies train members of their own staff to become word processing operators. Secretaries, typists, and other staff members are generally chosen to learn word processing skills because of their familiarity with company policies and procedures, equipment, training techniques, and work schedules.

Like college-level programs, company training programs vary considerably. Some employers develop their own in-house training programs. These can range from formal classroom instruction, to informal group classes, to one-on-one instruction. Other companies use programs and materials developed by the vendor from whom they purchased their system. Still others bring in outside consultants to do the training, or even encourage employees to become "self-taught" operators by reading equipment manuals. Most companies use some combination of these training methods.

A major advantage of company training is that it is free to the employee, paid for by the company. In addition, company-sponsored training ensures that you are learning to use the specific kind of equipment that you will be called upon to operate in your day-to-day work.

Before committing yourself to a company training program, make sure that the training is adequate. This can often be determined by talking to other operators and to the manager who coordinates the training effort.

Equipment-Vendor Training

Many word processing equipment vendors offer training to companies that lease or purchase their systems. Generally, the contract stipulates that the vendor will provide a certain amount of training to the purchaser's employees.

If you are chosen for vendor training, you can expect to be sent off-site to the vendor's facilities for training, or taught on your company's premises by a training representative of the vendor. In either case, training usually lasts for a relatively short period of time and must be supplemented by additional on-the-job training.

Like company training, vendor training is paid for by your employer, and you have the advantage of learning the system that you will be operating on a day-to-day basis.

Business and Secretarial School Training

The majority of business and secretarial schools now offer courses in word processing in addition to their regular curricula. An advantage of these programs is that they are often relatively brief (one year or less) and can be enrolled in at varying times of the year.

Business and secretarial schools also vary considerably in the size and quality of the word processing operation, reputation, and cost. You should personally visit any school that you are considering and talk to both students and administrators before signing a contract. When evaluating business and secretarial school word processing programs, make sure that the schools are licensed by a state educational agency. This ensures that, at minimum, the school's operations meet basic state standards.

Training Through Temporary Help Services

In an effort to satisfy the overwhelming market demand for temporary word processing personnel, a number of temporary help services now conduct word processing training for qualified individuals. Those chosen for training are registered with the service, have an interest in word processing, and meet certain minimum requirements.

Applicants are closely screened before being accepted for WP training. Screening generally covers typing skills, spelling, grammar, and communication skills. If you are accepted for training, you will learn one or more word processing systems that are located right at the temporary service's offices. In many cases, hands-on equipment training will be coupled with some amount of conceptual training. Temporary help services do not charge a fee for word processing training. However, you must agree to work for the service for a certain minimum number of hours in exchange for your training.

Obtaining WP training from a temporary help service has a number of advantages. First, the training is free, except for your time commitment to the service. Second, jobs obtained through the service can get you much needed experience and exposure to different types of businesses. In fact, some temporary WP employees have been asked to stay on permanently at businesses where they have proven their professionalism and willingness to work. Third, you can often be trained on more than one system, which makes you more marketable.

Other Sources of Training

Other training options do exist. Investigate adult continuing education programs, technical schools, and vocational rehabilitation programs. Also, some local community groups now sponsor word processing seminars.

Finally, you can always teach yourself the fundamentals of word processing. If you have access to word processing equipment and are willing to invest the time, it can be done. However, if you have the option, enroll in a formal program.

SELF-EVALUATION

Before you commit yourself to a word-processing training program, take some time to do a complete self-assessment. In particular, seriously evaluate whether or not you have the personal attributes and technical skills that are necessary for a successful word processing career. These qualifications were discussed in detail in Chapter 4.

Personal Traits

Professionalism
Interest in word processing
Dependability
Ability to handle pressure
Concentration
Human-relations skills
Task orientation

Technical Skills

Typing skills
Interest in machines
English language skills
Ability to read, follow
          & interpret directions

A WP career is not for everyone. However, if you feel that you have what it takes, you are ready to become a part of the exciting field of word processing.

GETTING EXPERIENCE

Getting hands-on word processing experience is an integral part of your individual training program. No matter how good your formal training program, you need to get experience in order to sharpen your skills. Not only will experience make you a more efficient WP operator, it will make you more marketable as you compete with other experienced operators for more interesting, higher paying WP positions.

There are a variety of ways to get experience, even while you are still training. You can apply for part-time positions and temporary jobs. Check your local newspaper, or register with a temporary service. You can even hire yourself out as a free-lance operator. There are many businesses and individuals willing to pay for one-time or short-term word processing help. You might even decide to volunteer your services to a worthwhile organization in exchange for machine time. Finally, if your school offers internships, you should try to get one.

The bottom line is to get experience, and many more employment doors will be open to you.

CHAPTER 6

MAJOR EMPLOYERS OF WORD PROCESSING PERSONNEL

One of the most exciting aspects of a word processing career is the wide range of employment opportunities that it offers. Word processing skills are in demand in virtually every business category. Therefore, you can combine your interest in a particular field, such as law, health care, or banking, with your word processing skills to land a position that suits your interests.

Qualifications for word processing positions vary from one industry to the next and from one employer to the next. In general, entry-level word processing positions require, at minimum, a high school diploma, typing skills, and good command of the English language. Some companies are willing to provide word processing training; others will only hire skilled word processing operators. In some fields, such as law and medicine, a working knowledge of the appropriate technical jargon may be required.

In this chapter, we will be taking a look at some of the major employers of word processing personnel. In particular, we will examine WP opportunities in the following fields: law, health care, the financial industry, government, large corporations, suppliers of temporary help, and the insurance industry.

This list is far from complete, but it is a sampling of the range of word processing opportunities available to you.

At the end of this chapter, you will find profiles of three individuals who work in the word processing field. Their experiences provide a realistic portrait of WP positions in several industries.

LAW

Many members of the legal profession enjoy the advantages of word processing systems. Users include sole practitioners; private law firms; federal, state, and local courts and agencies; corporate legal departments; and public interest groups.

Why does the legal profession find word processing so attractive? The practice of law is paper-intensive and deadline oriented, two characteristics that make it a prime candidate for word processing. Complex legal documents such as contracts, wills, legal briefs, leases, testimonies, and agreements are produced in staggering numbers, and they must be produced accurately and on schedule. Many of these documents go through a number of drafts on their way to final copy. The text-editing capabilities of word processing equipment make it possible to make revisions with speed and accuracy.

Although revisions are common, a significant amount of the language in legal documents is standard (or ''boilerplate''). With word processing, key paragraphs and phrases that are used often can be stored and merged with variable text as needed.

Word processing also makes routine paperwork less tedious. Law offices report that they use their WP systems for correspondence, maintenance of docket-calendar control and client records, and billing.

Word processing opportunities in the legal field are common. Today, most legal organizations use some type of word processing system. Equipment ranges from electronic typewriters to highly sophisticated shared and distributed logic systems. Word processing organizations range from one-person operations to large word processing departments. Some WP organizations work around-the-clock and even employ part-time workers as needed to share the heavy work load and maximize equipment efficiency.

Because of the demanding nature of legal work, employers are looking for highly skilled word processing operators, or trainable typists, who can handle detail work and are willing to work long, hard hours. The rewards can be excellent. In general, the legal profession pays above-average salaries and is known for its excellent benefits.

HEALTH CARE

The health-care profession also enjoys the benefits of word processing. WP systems can be found in many of the over 7,000 hospitals and clinics in this country and in the offices of numerous doctors, dentists, and veterinarians in private practice. As health-care costs continue to soar, word processing systems will become even more prevalent as individuals and organizations try to find ways to cut costs and become more competitive.

Word processors serve a variety of uses in the health-care field. They are used to store and update patients' medical records; to handle appointments, billing, and insurance reports; and to assist medical professionals in putting together reports, studies, and articles. Much routine correspondence (such as appointment reminders, introductions of new health-care services, and fundraising efforts) can also be handled efficiently with stored lists and common texts.

Word processing opportunities in the health-care field are good. Positions require strong word processing skills and may require familiarity with medical terminology.

THE FINANCIAL INDUSTRY

Financial institutions, such as banks, credit unions, and finance companies, vary considerably in the ways that they conduct their business affairs. However, one characteristic seems common to all: they are paper-intensive organizations that produce an abundance of written and numerical information. For most of these institutions, record keeping is automated and tends to be accomplished by large, computer-based systems that perform both word processing and data processing functions. Word processing is used to maintain detailed financial records; to produce newsletters, brochures and training manuals; and to correspond with potential and actual customers.

Like many industries today, the financial industry is highly competitive. Word processing helps companies to attract and keep customers by providing them with excellent service. For example, word processing allows banks to automatically notify customers about the status of their savings and checking accounts and about new and improved services. In addition, word processing makes it possible to efficiently and economically send out mass mailings to attract new customers and to develop new sources of capital.

The financial industry is an exciting place for WP personnel. The industry relies heavily on sophisticated computer equipment and depends on skilled professionals to keep the systems up and running.

Many financial institutions have large word processing organizations that employ the full range of word processing personnel. Qualifications for word processing positions in the financial industry include good word processing skills; an interest in working with numbers; and accuracy, honesty, and discretion. Opportunities for advancement are excellent because of the industry's heavy reliance on office automation technology.

GOVERNMENT ORGANIZATIONS

Federal, state, and local government organizations are also major users of word processing systems. Because the range of services that these organizations provide is so vast, so are the word processing opportunities. A government word processing job might involve working in fields as diverse as personnel, law, health and welfare, education, housing, or transportation, among others.

In recent years, government organizations have become increasingly reliant on word processing systems. This is because WP helps them become more productive and cut costs, two major goals of all government bureaucracies.

In general, standard procedures exist for locating and applying for government jobs. At the federal level, contact your local federal job information center for information about WP employment opportunities and application procedures. At the state and local levels, government personnel agencies can point you in the right direction. If possible, use personal contacts such as friends and family members already employed by the government to find out about opportunities and to get a foot in the door.

Qualifications for government word processing positions vary. Generally, good typing skills and adequate verbal and clerical aptitude can land you an entry-level position. Once you are in the system, opportunities for advancement are very good. With the right amount of education and experience, you can advance to professional and administrative government positions.

LARGE CORPORATIONS

What was hailed not so long ago as the office of the future is fast becoming the present reality for many of the nation's businesses. The primary catalyst for this change is sophisticated electronic equipment such as word processors and microcomputers. Almost all (98%) of the nation's largest firms (those on the Fortune 1300 list) already own some type of electronic equipment. When it comes to future job market prospects, more of these companies plan to hire employees with word processing skills than any other type of management support staff.*

This is the exciting conclusion of the *Kelly Report on People in the Electronic Office,* a study of the state of automation in Fortune 1300 companies. More specifically, the report notes that 95 percent of the companies surveyed have some type of word processing system in place. Therefore, if you are interested in working for a large corporation, you will find that many word processing opportunities exist.

Today, word processing systems are found in practically all types of corporations. Manufacturers, marketing organizations, publishing companies, transportation firms, oil giants, and drug companies are just a few of the many industries that rely heavily on WP technology. These industries report using their systems for

The Kelly Report on People in the Electronic Offices, p. 1. Courtesy of Kelly Services, Inc., 999 West Big Beaver Road, Troy, MI 48084.

customer records and contacts, correspondence, billing, large mailings, customer service, public relations, corporate planning, reports, contracts, and financial records. The list goes on and on.

Given the wide variety of WP applications used by businesses, it is not surprising that word processing systems are often found throughout the corporate organization. As a word processing employee, you might find yourself working in departments such as personnel, legal, marketing, operations, customer service, or corporate planning. Or you might find yourself on the team of a large, centralized word processing organization, performing a variety of word processing applications.

Corporate word processing opportunities are excellent. Virtually all large companies are committed to office automation as a means of improving worker productivity and increasing the speed and accuracy of operations. And word processing systems are a primary means of accomplishing these goals. Studies indicate that the majority of large corporations fill word processing vacancies primarily by training their own staff, and that most training takes place in house. Therefore, if you are already employed by a company with word processing equipment and you are interested in learning the system, your chances of being trained by your employer are very good.

Spin-off career opportunities for corporate word processing personnel are also excellent. Many operators move on to supervisory WP positions and other computer-related positions such as computer programmer, systems analyst, and equipment technician.

Many corporations pay above-average word processing salaries. When evaluating various companies, look at the size of the word processing operation, advancement potential, salary, benefits, and work environment to see if they meet your expectations.

TEMPORARY AGENCIES

Many businesses, at one time or another, require temporary help. Temporary services help companies to meet their short-term word processing needs by providing them with temporary word-processing employees. Temporaries fill in as vacation replacements, during peak work loads and rush jobs, and on one-time or short-term projects.

Whether you are an aspiring word processing operator or a skilled word processing professional, there are a number of reasons to consider registering with a temporary employment service. First, working at a variety of temporary jobs is an excellent way to gain valuable experience and to learn about different types of businesses. Second, temporary work gives you the option of saying "no" when you cannot or do not want to work. Most people with permanent jobs do not have this luxury. Third, temporary assignments can be taken while you are in-between jobs or on vacation from your regular work. For example, many teachers, college students, and others work as "temps" during their free time. Fourth, some temporary services provide word processing training to qualified individuals with an interest in the field. This can be a fast and inexpensive way to learn basic word processing skills. (See Chapter 5.)

The demand for temporary word-processing employees is good. Temporary services are actively seeking experienced word-processing professionals, newly trained WP operators, and WP trainees.

The financial rewards for temporary work are very good and increase with experience. On the average, temporary WP employees earn a higher hourly wage than temporary secretaries, typists, and other office support personnel.

THE INSURANCE INDUSTRY

Do you have an interest in the insurance industry? Word processors and other sophisticated automation systems are now standard equipment in most insurance companies, large and small. Without word processing, most of these companies could not survive in the highly competitive insurance market.

By their very nature, insurance companies produce tremendous quantities of information and paperwork. Word processors are used to store and update information on customer policies and claims, and to maintain records of types of coverage available, associated premiums, and payment schedules. In addition, they are used to send out prospecting letters, billing notices, and notices of changes in coverage.

What kinds of word processing opportunities exist in the insurance industry? The number and variety of WP positions in the insurance industry are growing. WP personnel assist insurance agents and management-level personnel in handling their paperwork. Many larger insurance companies employ the full range of WP personnel to meet the tremendous work load. In addition, a growing number of insurance agents now have word processing equipment right at their desks to help them operate more efficiently. As an insurance agent, therefore, you might well be expected to operate word processing equipment on a day-to-day basis.

Good word processing skills and an interest in working with both numbers and people are prerequisites for a career in the insurance industry. Salaries and benefits vary considerably from one company to the next. Be sure to compare companies before taking a position.

INDIVIDUAL PROFILES

Natalie Urich
Health-Care Industry

Little Company of Mary Hospital is a 268-bed acute care facility in southern California, run by the Sisters of the Little Company of Mary, a congregation of Catholic nuns. During the last few years, the hospital has installed a number of stand-alone word processing units and microcomputers with word processing capabilities. This equipment plays an important role in the day-to-day operations of the hospital. The medical records department, the pharmacy, and the health education department all use the equipment. In addition, word processors are located at several secretarial workstations.

Natalie Urich is employed as administrative secretary to the hospital's director of development and community relations. Because her position requires her to produce a large volume and variety of paperwork, she was one of the first Little Company of Mary employees to be trained on the hospital's word processing equipment. Natalie readily admits that she was initially skeptical of the new equipment and its capabilities. Today, however, she has a word processor right at her desk and relies on it for most of her daily output.

Natalie's primary responsibility is to support the director of development and community relations. One of the director's major responsibilities is hospital fundraising. With the help of her word processor, Natalie produces fundraising letters and other related materials. The hospital's mailing list is stored on disks and is used selectively for various fundraising efforts. Word processing allows Natalie to personalize every letter that is sent out of the hospital without having to individually type each one. As Natalie explains,

"The word processor saves time and results in a more professional-looking product. It helps present a much better image of the hospital."

Natalie highly recommends word processing training to anyone interested in a secretarial career. She explains, "In hospitals and other businesses, the opportunities for an individual with a word processing background are endless."

Ronnie Stifter
Aerospace Industry

Ronnie Stifter is employed by an aerospace company in southern California. She is currently supervisor of computer training. In that position, her primary responsibility is to coordinate the various in-house training programs that are offered to employees in her area. In particular, much of her work involves computer training of employees, including instruction on the use of word processing equipment and software.

As a training specialist for a large corporation, Ronnie has been able to combine two interests: teaching and computers. Prior to joining her present employer, she worked for 13 years as a teacher at the preschool, kindergarten, and junior high school levels. Although she loved teaching, Ronnie decided to leave the profession to try her hand at something new and different. She found that opportunity in the aerospace industry.

During the last eight to ten years, Ronnie has held a number of positions. She worked for a while in finance and eventually became a computer programmer. (She went back to school part-time and received a certificate in applications programming from UCLA.)

While Ronnie was working as a programmer, a new word processing system was introduced; she was asked to learn the system and conduct a small amount of training. She did, and her training career "just naturally evolved" from that point on. As more office automation devices were added, more training was needed, and Ronnie often did it.

Ronnie believes that her teaching background has helped her to be a more effective corporate-level trainer. She points out that word processing, in particular, is one area where that background has been a real asset. "Just because you know word processing doesn't mean that you can teach it. . . . There's a skill to getting people to understand the system and to feel comfortable with it."

In her day-to-day work, Ronnie uses word processing, teaches it, and consults with other users who need her assistance. She particularly enjoys the consulting aspect of her work. She explains:

> When you work with users, you have a much better idea of how they need to use the system, which means that sometimes we change our training program based on what we see people using it for...or what their needs are.

The users who work with Ronnie come from a variety of backgrounds. Some have a good deal of computer experience; others have none. Ronnie believes that the real keys to success in the word-processing field are a positive attitude and lots of hands-on experience. Those who keep an open mind and are willing to learn tend to be successful. And there is certainly no substitute for experience. Ronnie explains:

> I think the only way to learn anything, whether you are going to be the trainer or not, is to use it. . . . You have to experiment, and if you are afraid to experiment, I think you lose a lot. At any training classes you go to, you are not going to learn everything there is to know about a system. You are going to get the groundwork so that you can leave and do basic things and go on from there. You are not going to be

an expert. That is why on-the-job training and hands-on experience are so important.

What personal qualities does Ronnie think make for a successful word-processing trainer? Lots of equipment experience and a true interest in teaching are minimum requirements.

Sharon Morrill
The Legal Profession

Sharon Morrill has been operating word processing equipment in a legal environment for over ten years. As a legal secretary in the fast-paced Washington, D.C., corporate law market, Sharon's responsibilities include typing, filing, and other administrative tasks, such as the coordination of large mailings and photocopying.

Sharon explains that the position of legal secretary can be a very demanding one. Her present employer, for example, requires typing skills of 80 words-per-minute and shorthand or dictation equipment experience. In addition, strong English skills (spelling, grammar, and punctuation), a legal background, and organizational ability are essential.

In her present position, Sharon works for two attorneys, one partner, and one associate. Like all of the secretaries at the law firm, she has her own word processor, an IBM model, which she was taught to operate by a fellow employee. Sharon puts all of her typewritten work on the word processor, from one-page memos to 50-page legal briefs. Because of the heavy typing work load, Sharon estimates that she spends 75 percent of her work day, on the average, at the word processor. While the equipment "makes revisions easier and allows you to easily produce a perfect product," Sharon also feels that "working in front of a machine all day [can] become boring, repetitive, and not challenging."

Sharon sees little opportunity for advancement in her present job. Given the firm's organizational structure, "you are either a lawyer, paralegal, or secretary." Therefore, Sharon aspires to leave the traditional secretarial job market and start her own home-based word processing business. In her own words:

> I plan to start my own word processing business working out of my home. My first prospective customer is a real estate agent who wants to send out form letters to potential clients. I also may get some work through my brother-in-law, who is a technical manager for an office equipment company. I also plan to advertise at the University of Maryland, which is five minutes from my home. I hope to work three or four hours a day, preferably in the evenings when my husband can watch our daughter. Several years ago, I purchased an early model word processor. In the beginning, I can use that machine. If my business picks up, I would like to buy a sophisticated word processor.

Given her strong work experience and good business sense, Sharon should be very successful in her business venture.

CHAPTER 7

SPIN-OFF CAREERS

What other career opportunities are open to WP operators? If you are looking to advance beyond the WP operator ranks, you will find that your word processing background gives you an added advantage in the job market. You have a technical skill and experience, two qualities that are highly regarded by all employers.

There are a wide variety of spin-off careers that you might want to consider. Not surprisingly, many WP operators advance within the traditional word processing structure. They move on to positions as WP supervisors, managers, proofreaders, and trainers. Others find employment with WP equipment vendors in fields such as sales, marketing support, equipment service, and training. Less traditional spin-off possibilities include WP consulting, teaching, and operating your own home-based WP business.

When considering spin-off opportunities, it is important to keep in mind that word processing is just one aspect of office automation. Computers also serve a variety of other uses in businesses. Opportunities in the computer field are vast, and some word processing personnel naturally progress to these positions. We will be looking at two spin-off possibilities in the computer field: systems analysis and computer programming.

If you are interested in a more comprehensive look at computer careers, take some time to review the following books:

The Computer Careers Handbook,
    by Connie Winkler.

The Fast Track to the Top Jobs in Computer Careers,
    by Peter Muller.

Opportunities in Data Processing Careers,
    by Norman N. Noerper.

Without a doubt, you will find many more career opportunities available to you as your level of education and work experience increase. However, if you are a relative newcomer to the word processing field with a limited amount of education, this should not deter you. With a high school diploma and technical word processing skills, it is still possible to spin off to other interesting positions.

Here are four suggestions for using your WP background to move on to new fields of endeavor:

- Try to switch careers within the company that presently employs you. This is your best bet for advancement. Internal promotions and lateral moves are common because many companies are willing to take a chance on employees who have already proven themselves in the business, even if their educational background and work experience are limited. If there are additional opportunities with your present employer, check them out.
- Use your professional contacts to find out about potential jobs. After working in the word processing field for a while, you will have developed a number of contacts (with principals within your own organization and vendor representatives, for example) who may be able to give you some job leads. Also,

do not overlook the assistance of friends and acquaintances who work for other companies that may be of interest to you.

- Regularly scan employment ads that are placed in the local newpaper by businesses. The ads will give you an idea of the types of jobs that are available and what qualifications you need to get them.
- Talk to employment agencies. Describe your background and aspirations. The agencies can give you valuable information about the current job market and how your credentials stack up in that market.

Before embarking on a new career, take some time to learn as much as you can about the field that interests you. If you are considering a career in computer programming, for example, go to your local library and read up on the subject. Talk to people who are already in that field. They can give you a realistic portrayal of what your day-to-day work would be like. If you have to go back to school for your new career, try to take one or two relevant courses while you are still at your present position to make sure that your interest is well-founded.

Most important of all, match yourself to the job. Determine the technical skills and personal attributes necessary for the position that interests you, and make sure that you have what it takes.

In the rest of this chapter, we will be taking a look at some of the more popular spin-off careers for word processing personnel. These include:

Word processing supervision/management
Sales
Marketing support
Equipment service
Teaching
Computer programming
Systems analysis

Consulting
Home-based businesses.

For each of these positions, we will discuss the nature of the job, qualifications, salaries, and the employment outlook.

MANAGEMENT

One of the most obvious and natural spin-off careers for word processing operators is WP management. As outlined in Chapter 3, word processing managers oversee the entire word processing operation of a company or of a WP division within a company. Specific duties include developing procedures for word processing operations; selecting, directing, and guiding WP personnel; distributing the work load; maintaining liaison with upper-level management; and keeping up-to-date on new WP equipment and procedures. In addition, WP managers are often responsible for the WP budget, production reports, training schedules, and coordination of activities with the administrative side of the organization.

Many WP managers start out as word processing operators and gradually assume supervisory and management positions. Others are formally educated in management techniques and learn word processing on-the-job. If you are interested in eventually joining the WP management ranks, it would be to your advantage to get some formalized management training. Ideally, you should obtain a college degree, while concentrating on courses in management, human relations, communications, and word processing concepts and operations, at a minimum.

Because the position of WP manager is so demanding, employers are looking for individuals with word processing expertise, lots of hands-on experience, the ability to work well under pressure, a good educational background, excellent training and communications skills, and strong, well-developed interpersonal skills.

WP managers earn an average of $25,000–$30,000 per year. Opportunities for advancement can be excellent. Some WP managers go on to oversee a company's entire information processing operation. Others move on to management positions outside of the word/information processing field. Independent consulting is another viable and profitable option for the highly skilled WP manager.

SALES

Do you have an outgoing personality and strong communications skills? If so, you may be well suited for a career in word processing sales. A position in WP sales involves selling WP equipment and/or supplies to businesses and individuals. Salespeople work for WP equipment vendors and are usually assigned a specific territory or industry to call upon. Their job is to assess a potential customer's word processing needs and to find a system that meets those needs. They then prepare a proposal for the customer that outlines the recommended system, its advantages, and associated costs. The salesperson's ultimate goal is to use his or her persuasive abilities to make a sale.

Qualifications for sales positions vary considerably. Although a college degree is generally not a prerequisite, it is becoming more and more common, especially in larger companies. Some companies require an associate degree or four-year degree in marketing or sales. Most vendors prefer that you have prior sales experience; it does not necessarily have to be in the word processing field, although some computer background is preferred. Once hired, sales representatives usually attend some formal or informal sales training classes that are intended to teach the vendor's specific approach to selling.

If you are interested in a career in sales, you should have excellent verbal and written communications skills, strong human relations skills, a sharp appearance, stamina, and self-confidence. Without a doubt, you should enjoy selling and be able to handle all of the pressures associated with such a demanding position.

Opportunities in WP sales are excellent. However, it is important to point out that competition among salespeople is fierce, and many individuals do not succeed in the field. If you are successful, a sales career can be very lucrative. Salaries are usually based on experience and individual performance. That is, you earn a base salary plus commissions on your sales. Incomes for successful salespeople range from $25,000 to $60,000, and over, per year. Some have made as much as $100,000 or more per year.

Advancement potential for members of the sales force is also excellent. Successful salespeople often join the management ranks of vendor companies because of their detailed knowledge of the WP market and the company's customer base.

MARKETING SUPPORT

Marketing Support Representatives (MSRs) are also employed by word processing equipment vendors. The primary function of MSRs is to support the sales force. They do this by demonstrating the features and applications of WP equipment to new and potential customers, training new users on their systems, and consulting with customers about how they can better use their systems or how they can solve an equipment problem.

Many MSRs come from the ranks of word processing operators. Because of their own hands-on experience with WP equipment, they are better able to understand customer needs and to effectively teach others how to use the system. Some MSRs have a teaching background that they apply to their position. This, however, is usually not a prerequisite.

Some of the qualities that vendors look for in their MSRs include excellent communications skills, an understanding of people and their equipment problems and needs, teaching skills, persuasiveness, tactfulness, and diplomacy. Of course, a word processing background helps.

MSRs work for a straight salary. Beginning salaries range from $20,000 to $25,000 per year. Salaries, on the average, are in the $25,000-$35,000 per year range.

Many MSRs go on to careers in sales, and some move on to management positions in vendor organizations.

EQUIPMENT SERVICE

Equipment Service Representatives (ESRs) work for the repair or service departments of word processing equipment vendors. The responsibilities of ESRs include installing new equipment at customer locations and servicing existing equipment. Servicing can involve routine preventive maintenance or emergency repairs. ESRs first become proficient at common repairs. Over time, they may specialize in more difficult repair problems.

As you might well expect, ESRs have a background in electronics and equipment repair, and they are mechanically inclined. Although it is generally not a requirement, some ESRs have two- or four-year college degrees. Most employers of ESRs conduct their own training programs. Some have company repair schools.

Others conduct intensive on-the-job training. Because WP equipment is changing all the time, many ESRs attend brush-up classes and seminars on a regular basis to keep up-to-date about their equipment.

Because ESRs are the customer's primary interface with the vendor during installation and after training, they need to be quick and responsive to the customer's needs. The ability to handle pressure is essential, as ESRs are usually needed only when something has gone wrong with the equipment and the customer is losing valuable time and money. Other important traits would include initiative, organizational ability, interpersonal skills, and problem-solving ability.

Typical of other positions in the computer field, the employment outlook for ESRs is excellent. ESRs make an average of $20,000–$30,000 per year. A background as a service representative can eventually lead to a career in sales, engineering, or even research and development.

TEACHING

Do you have a teaching background or an interest in teaching? Word processing instructors are in demand as the number of facilities that offer WP training continues to grow. WP instructors are needed in a variety of settings. Teaching positions are available at four-year and community colleges, private business and secretarial schools, vendor companies, and private companies that conduct their own in-house WP training.

Many WP instructors have an A.A. or a B.A. in a field such as business education, business administration, or office occupations. Many also have teaching and/or word processing work experience. In some instances, especially in business and secretarial schools, relevant work experience can be substituted for certain educational requirements.

WP instructors should enjoy teaching and working with people, have the ability to simplify seemingly complex material, and be thoroughly familiar with several word processing systems. In addition, they should have strong presentation skills, and be patient and generous with their time.

The job outlook for word processing instructors is good. More and more schools are adding WP courses to their curricula, more businesses are investing in WP systems, and more vendors are offering WP training.

Salaries vary by region and industry. On the average, a WP instructor can expect to make $25,000–$30,000 per year. However, some trainers earn as little as $15,000 per year, and others make as much as $50,000 or more.

COMPUTER PROGRAMMING

Computer programs are sets of instructions that tell a computer what to do. Computer programmers design computer programs and modify existing ones to better suit user needs. This involves taking a problem description (a routine that someone wants the computer to perform) and translating that description into a program written in computer language.

Many computer programmers begin their careers as trainees and gradually progress to more difficult assignments and higher-level programming positions. Many companies have programmer career ladders, offering opportunities for senior programmers, team leaders, and programming managers, among others.

Qualifications for computer programming positions are getting more stringent all the time. Today, many companies (especially the larger ones) require, at minimum, a bachelor's degree in a field such as data processing, computer science, accounting, or business administration. An associate degree in data processing or some course work in the field can still land you an entry-level position, but such opportunities are very limited. Some companies provide on-the-job training to qualified employees with little or no programming background. However, this is becoming less common as the number of trained programmers in the work force continues to increase. In addition, there are numerous technical schools that offer computer programming courses. Colleges and technical schools, however, can now afford to be choosy. There are often many more applicants than spaces available because of the increased interest in the programming field.

What traits should a computer programmer possess? Successful programmers tend to have many of the following characteristics: creativity, problem-solving ability, a cooperative attitude, detail orientation, deadline orientation, the ability to handle stress, adaptability, neatness, orderliness, flexibility, the ability to work as part of a team, willingness to work long hours, a logical mind.

Because computers are now standard business equipment, employment opportunities for computer programmers exist in practically every type of business. The United States Department of Labor, Bureau of Labor Statistics, reports:

> Employment of programmers is expected to grow much faster that the average for all occupations through the year 2000 as computer usage expands. . . . The need for programmers will increase as businesses, government, schools, and scientific organizations seek new applications for computers and improvements to the software already in use. Further automation of offices and factories, advances in health and medicine, and continuing scientific research will drive the growth of programmer employment.

Employment, however is not expected to grow as rapidly as in the past as improved software and programming techniques simplify or eliminate some programming tasks. The greater use of packaged software that can meet the needs of many users also may moderate the growth in demand for applications programmers.

Job prospects should be good for college graduates who are familiar with a variety of programming languages, particularly newer languages that apply to computer networking, data base management, and artificial intelligence.

On the average, computer programmers make an annual salary of $22,000–$40,000. Entry-level positions can start as low as $16,000. With the right amount of training and experience, a good programmer can make $50,000 + .

Advancement potential for programmers is excellent. Many go on to positions as senior programmers, systems analysts, and data processing managers.

SYSTEMS ANALYSIS

Like programmers, systems analysts also work closely with computers. Their job is to develop ways to improve the organization's use of its computer equipment. They do this by helping equipment users articulate their needs and by recommending ways that the computer system can meet those needs. In some instances, if the present equipment's capabilities are insufficient to solve a major problem, systems analysts may get involved in studying and recommending new equipment. Once a solution has been developed, they often work with the programming staff to implement the solution.

Because systems analysts work closely with equipment users, they must be highly informed about the different types of work that the company does. In addition, they must be well versed on the capabilities of the company's computer system. They should also be aware of new technologies that are available to the company.

Systems analysts are generally considered to be a step above programmers on the career ladder. Therefore, they tend to have more experience and education than the average programmer. Today, a four-year college degree and some computer experience are the norm for most systems analyst positions. Graduate degrees are becoming more and more common. Courses in computer programming, word processing, data processing, and computer operations are helpful. Also, systems analysts should have a broad business background in order to understand the special needs/problems of system users.

Characteristics of successful systems analysts include the ability to think clearly and logically, strong written and verbal communications skills, analytical skills, the ability to work well with individuals from a variety of backgrounds, good business sense, and a background in computer programming (although this is not always required).

The job outlook for systems analysts is very good. The United States Department of Labor, Bureau of Labor Statistics, reports:

> Employment of systems analysts is expected to grow much faster than the average for all occupations through the year 2000....College graduates who have had courses in computer programming, systems analysis, and other data processing areas as well as training or experience in an applied field should enjoy good prospects for employment. Persons without a college degree and college graduates unfamiliar with data processing will face keen competition from the large number of experienced workers seeking jobs as systems analysts.

Salaries for systems analysts are excellent. They average $27,000–$45,000 per year. A top-notch systems analyst can earn much more.

Advancement potential for systems analysts is also very good. Many go on to managerial positions in the data processing field or to other areas of the organization.

CONSULTING

Word processing consultants are individuals who market their considerable WP expertise to businesses, often on a free-lance basis. WP consultants are hired by businesses for any number of reasons. They can provide knowledgeable advice about which WP system a company should install, how the equipment can best be utilized, and what types of training the company should invest in. Also, they are often employed to persuade upper-level management of the benefits of word processing. In most cases, consultants are only employed by a company for a specified period of time or until a specific project is completed.

Consultants may work for a variety of industries, or they may specialize in a particular industrial field. Some work independently, while other are members of consulting groups or companies.

Qualifications for consultants include word processing expertise, familiarity with a wide variety of WP equipment, creativity and objectivity, and a strong background in data processing and management. Although a degree is not as important as experience and knowledge, it certainly makes the consultant more marketable.

Experienced WP consultants can command excellent fees, and at the present time, there is a real demand for their services.

HOME-BASED WORD PROCESSING BUSINESSES

Do you enjoy your independence? Would you like to be self-employed? If so, do not overlook the possibility of using your word processing skills to start your own home-based WP business. In ever increasing numbers, skilled WP operators with business know-how are choosing to leave the traditional job market and open up their own home-based word processing operations. Their clients include companies with an overflow of work; companies without word processing equipment; students, professors, and writers with papers to be typed; and small businesses with little or no support staff.

In order to open up shop, you need to have the following: your own word processing equipment (which is sophisticated enough to meet your clients' needs), top-notch word processing skills, marketing skills (to market yourself and your service), and business contacts. Good business sense will come in handy for determining fees and handling clients on a professional basis. In addition, you need to have drive, ambition, a commitment to your business, and management skills.

The advantages of working for yourself are many. First and foremost, you get to be your own boss. You do not have to answer to anyone but yourself and your clients. You can set your own hours and work at your own speed. You can chart your own future. If you want your business to stay small, it can. If you want to expand your operations, the sky can be the limit.

Potential disadvantages should also be considered. As a self-employed worker, you do not get paid vacations or the other benefits associated with traditional jobs. Also, you must attract regular business or you do not get paid. If your marketing skills are weak, you become ill, or your clients no longer need your services, your business will probably not survive.

However, it is possible to surmount these potential difficulties with the proper attitude and know-how. If you are serious about working out of your home, take some time to read an excellent book on the subject: *Word Processing Profits at Home* by Peggy Glenn (Huntington Beach, CA: Aames-Allen Publishing Company, 1983).

Salary potential as a self-employed worker depends on how much or how little you want to work. Even on a part-time basis, home-based word processing can be very lucrative.

CHAPTER 8

TRENDS IN WORD PROCESSING AND OFFICE AUTOMATION

Most discussions of trends in office automation technology include predictions about "the office of the future." In a very real sense, however, the office of the future is already in place in many of our nation's businesses, and it is right around the corner for many others. Today, sophisticated office automation systems, capable of a broad assortment of functions, are depended on by many businesses to help them be more creative and productive. These automated systems are rapidly becoming indispensable office tools, essential to the efficient operation of businesses of all types and sizes.

Current office automation systems, such as word processing, have proven very effective in increasing worker productivity and containing office costs, two critical business goals. Given these results, it is not surprising that most businesses support additional research and development in the OA field. This wholehearted commitment to OA by the business community provides manufacturers with the impetus they need to improve on current technology.

As a result, substantial progress continues to be made in the office automation field. Exciting innovations are being developed and marketed all the time; and just as quickly as new developments are introduced, even more astonishing advances are announced.

In the word processing field alone, many improvements continue to be made to current systems to make them more efficient as well as more compatible with other office automation technology. In fact, the trend in the design of word processing and other OA equipment is toward a "systems approach" to the workplace. Manufacturers are now developing and marketing automated tools that work in harmony, not at odds, with one another. Today, businesses can purchase "office automation packages," instead of having to buy many individual and often incompatible pieces of automated equipment. These OA packages are designed to meet the many and varied computer needs of companies, including word processing.

Not too long ago, many people predicted that office automation would eventually result in the elimination of most office jobs. Although growth in the field has begun to slow, word processing and other automated systems continue to create many interesting, new career options for office workers. As we have seen, a variety of opportunities abound in all types of organizations; and because of the dynamic nature of the OA field, additional opportunities will continue to unfold.

As an aspiring WP professional, you should be familiar with the latest trends and opportunities in word processing and office automation. Why? Such knowledge will help you to better clarify your own career goals and will make you a more informed business professional. In the remainder of this chapter, we will be taking a brief look at some of the exciting advances that are being made in word processing and office automation technology. In addition, we will see what impact those advances are having on business organizational patterns and employment opportunities in the WP field. Unfortunately, it is beyond the scope of this book to discuss all recent trends. However, those that are discussed are expected to have a major impact on the future direction of WP and OA.

MULTIFUNCTION WORKSTATIONS

Throughout this book, our discussion of WP systems has centered on the stand-alone, single-purpose word processor with full video display screen. This machine is only capable of performing WP tasks. However, current sales figures indicate that the trend in the business community is away from single-function machines and toward multifunction workstations.

Multifunction workstations are computerized systems that are capable of performing a variety of functions in addition to word processing. For example, at a multifunction workstation, the same terminal might be used for word processing, data processing, electronic mail, graphics, and much more.

How is all of this accomplished? Some multifunction workstations are fully capable computers that have been programmed to perform numerous tasks in addition to word processing. Other terminals are essentially ''dumb;'' that is, they must be connected to a mainframe or other host computer that serves as a centralized data bank and also provides individual terminals with logic and storage power.

Because of their versatility, multifunctional systems are not only found at secretarial workstations. Many businesses locate them throughout the organization, where they can be used by managers, writers, analysts, and other members of the office staff who need to access their capabilities.

COMMUNICATING TERMINALS

Today, many word processing and multifunctional terminals are capable of communicating with one another. Communication is accomplished by the transmission of data at high speeds by electronic means, usually using telephone lines or satellites. The equipment user keys information into a terminal in one location and, with the push of a button, sends it to a communicating terminal at another location. The receiving terminal stores the data and is able to print it out. All of these activities occur almost instantaneously.

With this technology, transmissions can occur over any distance—within an office building, within the same city, or between offices hundreds of miles apart. In the word processing field, this communications capability is often used to "share" work and data among operators or principals who are spread out at two or more locations.

A growing number of WP and multifunctional terminals are also electronically linked to the company's central computer system. In other words, individual terminals can communicate with the main computer. This permits terminal users to access the company's central data bank and, in some instances, to share the main computer's logic and storage power. With this capability, individual managers have access to computerized information as diverse as inventory records, personnel data, and sales forecasts.

Many terminals also have access to sources of data outside of the company. For a fee, terminals can communicate with external data banks, which offer such specialized information as stock market reports, general news, legal decisions, and much more. Use of these external information sources by businesses is on the rise because user fees are declining, and more terminals are becoming capable of accessing these data banks.

ELECTRONIC MAIL

Today, it is not always necessary to send mail by way of the post office or to have it hand delivered by a messenger. With a communicating terminal, you can send messages to other people by means of electronic signals rather than paper and ink.

In-house electronic mail systems are in place in numerous businesses. These systems make it possible for employees to exchange messages with one another. How do these systems work? The messages are transmitted electronically using a network of interconnected communicating terminals. In traditional offices, employees have wooden, plastic, or metal in-baskets on their desks for receiving incoming mail and messages. In companies with electronic mail systems, employees have electronic in-baskets, which list all messages that have arrived at their terminal. At the touch of a button, the messages appear on the VDT. After each message has been read, it can be deleted from the system, filed for future reference, returned to the sender with a reply, or routed to another employee.

Internal electronic mail systems allow all of the members of an organization to be more productive. A significant amount of time is saved because employees no longer play "telephone tag," exchanging calls back and forth as they try to reach one another by telephone. In addition, electronic mail systems reduce paperwork, thus allowing workers to be more efficient and more productive.

Today, companies like Western Union make it possible for customers to use their computer terminals to send messages, or "mail," electronically to people around the world. With the push of a button, it is possible to send telex and TWX messages, mailgrams, computer letters, and telegrams quickly and effortlessly.

OPTICAL CHARACTER READERS

An optical character reader (OCR) is a piece of equipment that scans text that has been typed on a standard typewriter and converts the characters in that text into electronic signals which can be recorded onto magnetic disks or tapes. In essence, an OCR automatically converts a typewritten document into a form useable by a word processor, eliminating the need to have an equipment operator key the original document into the WP system.

For example, suppose you have just typed a three-page document on an electric typewriter. Now you realize that a lot of revisions are going to have to be made, and it would be very helpful to have the document on a word processor. With an OCR, it is possible to scan the typewritten copy and record it on magnetic tapes or disks. This eliminates the tedious task of retyping the document into a form acceptable to the word processor.

For many companies, investment in an optical character reader is very attractive. With an OCR, a company can continue to use standard office typewriters as the first step in the word processing cycle. Documents are typed on the typewriter, scanned by the OCR, then edited and formatted on WP equipment. With this capability, businesses can obtain the efficiencies of word processing, while investing in fewer costly WP systems.

VOICE-ACTIVATED WORD PROCESSING

The most time-consuming aspect of word processing is typing the original document into the WP system. The day is coming, however, when typing on a keyboard may be obsolete. Because voice-recognition technology is progressing so rapidly, it is realistic to predict that keyboards will eventually become a thing of the past and voice-activated word processing equipment will become commonplace.

In time, you will be able to "speak" to your word processor and have your words accurately converted into text on the WP screen. In fact, WP equipment capable of distinguishing words already exists in prototype. Much more research is needed, however, before such equipment becomes a practical reality. Machines would have to be able to understand a variety of speech patterns and accurately spell and punctuate before they could be widely used. Voice-recognition experts predict that day will come.

PORTABLE COMPUTERS

The trend in computer hardware development is toward more compact, multifunctional equipment. One manifestation of this trend is the portable computer, a lightweight system that is small enough to fit inside a briefcase. The small size enables people who travel to carry their computer with them and use it outside of the traditional office setting.

Two of the most frequent uses served by portable computers are word processing and communications. With a "lap-size" system, users can produce letters, memos, and other documents with ease. Then, using the communications capability of the equipment, those documents can be sent electronically, usually by means of telephone lines, to distant locations. This feature makes it possible for business people who are on the road to keep in touch with the home office, customers, and the company data base, even though they may be separated from one another by many miles. For example, the portable computer can be used by the travelling executive to "talk" to customers and members of the company staff; in addition, that same computer may provide the executive with corporate sales data, price lists, and even personal messages from the home office.

Portable systems vary greatly in terms of capabilities. Some are essentially "dumb" terminals; they are only capable of sending information, such as sales figures and other reports, to the home office. Other portable computers are much more sophisticated, capable of performing a wide range of business applications.

WORD PROCESSING IN THE HOME

In the not-too-distant future, multifunctional computers with word processing capabilities will be as commonplace in American households as televisions and telephones. In fact, personal computer systems (also referred to as home computer systems), ranging in price from several hundred to several thousand dollars, are already in place and serving a variety of uses in millions of American homes. Typically, home computers are used to play electronic games, balance the checkbook, and do simple word processing. However, more and more families are also using their systems for many of the same applications as businesses do, including detailed financial record keeping, list maintenance, sophisticated word processing, and business transactions, such as banking and bill paying.

It is predicted that by the year 2000, most families will depend on home computers to handle most of their day-to-day business, including bookkeeping, budgeting, bill paying, and all financial record keeping. Those same computers will also be used to maintain detailed lists of everything from phone numbers to birthdates, and to maintain inventories of household items such as books, magazines, tools, and even recipes. Undoubtedly, they will replace typewriters, making it easier for adults and children alike to be proficient "word processors."

Already, many elementary schools and high schools are introducing students to computers in the classroom. Soon, computers will be standard teaching aids, making the 3R's easier and more fun for students to learn. And as increasing numbers of children learn about and come to rely on computer technology, computers will find their way into more and more homes.

Home computers with communications capabilities already give consumers access to a wide variety of external data, such as stock market reports, weather information, and sports data. Eventually, every type of information imaginable will be available to home computer owners in seconds. In addition, families will be able to send most of their business and personal mail by computer and "communicate" electronically with people around the world.

These are only a few of the many exciting present and potential applications of home computers. The possibilities are endless, and researchers are hard at work typing to make them realities.

ORGANIZATIONAL TRENDS

As detailed in Chapter 3, the three most common organizational patterns that result when businesses implement word processing systems are centralized word processing, decentralized word processing, and word processing adapted to the traditional office structure. In the 1960s and 1970s, centralized word processing structures were undoubtedly the most popular. When businesses first invested in WP, many of them decided to establish separate word processing and administrative support centers to provide specialized support to the organization. As a result, word processing equipment was put in a central location and was operated only by the word processing staff.

With the trend toward a systems approach to the workplace and the growth of low-cost, multifunctional computer equipment, some of these businesses have begun to reassess their centralized word processing structures. Instead of isolating equipment in a central location, many businesses are choosing to place automated equipment throughout the office, where it can be used by secretaries, managers, technical writers, analysts, clerks, and anyone else who needs to access and process information. Today, a computer at one's workstation is often a status symbol, a sign that the user is computer literate and an information processor.

Even though many businesses are moving away from a totally centralized approach to word processing, most of them still hire full-time WP operators and other WP professionals to carry out and oversee large and complicated word processing tasks. These WP personnel often work closely with other equipment users in the organization to ensure the effective use of the WP system.

EMPLOYMENT TRENDS

What impact will all of these developments have on employment opportunities for word processing professionals? Because of their technical expertise, WP personnel will continue to enjoy a real advantage in the job market for many years to come. As employers continue to integrate newer and more sophisticated equipment into their OA systems, they will be looking for professionals who already have experience in an automated environment. Individuals with word processing skills will be in demand, and they will have many flexible career options available to them.

New positions for individuals with word processing backgrounds continue to unfold. Consultants, systems analysts and designers, equipment operators and technicians, trainers, supervisors, and more are needed in virtually every industry. Jobs that once were considered clerical, such as equipment operator, are becoming technical specialties. They generally require more education, but the payback comes in higher salaries and more opportunities for advancement. The greatest long-term opportunities exist for individuals who are well versed in several aspects of office automation technology, such as WP, data processing, and electronic mail systems.

In sum, the word processing and office automation fields will continue to offer many diverse and interesting career choices for years to come, and those careers will pay above-average salaries, offer challenge, and provide a strong foundation for professional growth and development.

CHAPTER 9

WHAT TO DO NEXT

Many people approach career planning haphazardly and, as a result, are dissatisfied with their work. This is unfortunate, especially considering the many hours that most of them spend at their jobs each day. You can avoid being another casualty of poor career planning by taking time to determine your word processing career goals and to map out a strategy for attaining them. By doing so, you will be ensuring yourself a satisfying and rewarding future in the WP job market.

This chapter offers some basic guidelines for engaging in WP career planning and job hunting. If you desire additional information or assistance, you should consult your local library. A number of excellent books provide step-by-step career guidance. For example, *What Color Is Your Parachute? A Practical Manual for Job-Hunters and Career Changers,* by Richard Nelson Bolles, is a widely acclaimed career planning guide, and there are many others.

DETERMINING YOUR CAREER GOALS

Before you start applying for word processing positions, it is important that you clarify your personal career goals. It is not enough to say that you want to be a word processing operator or an equipment technician. Your goals should be based on a clear understanding of your individual characteristics and how they match up with the job market that interests you. Once you have such an understanding, you will find it much easier to find a satisfying position in the job market.

Conducting a Personal Inventory

To get a better understanding of the types of work you may qualify for and enjoy, you should conduct a complete analysis of your interests, abilities, skills, and past accomplishments. Some of the questions you may want to consider include:

- What types of work do you enjoy doing? What types of work do you dislike? For example, do you like/dislike typing, filing, public speaking, managing people, managing projects, writing, working with equipment? Be specific.
- Do you have any special skills or abilities that you enjoy using? For example, are you good at understanding technical equipment?
- Do you enjoy working closely with other people, or do you prefer to work by yourself?
- Are you looking for a long-term career opportunity or a temporary position? Are you interested in growth potential?
- Do you enjoy responsibility? Are you looking for a position with responsibility?
- How well do you handle pressure? Do you want a position that involves a lot of pressure?
- What aspects of past jobs did you like/dislike?

- How do you rate your communications skills? Do you enjoy writing or public speaking?
- What is your educational background?

By studying your answers to questions such as these, you should begin to develop a better understanding of the kinds of work you should and should not consider. For example, a position as a WP equipment operator is probably not for you if you do not especially enjoy typing and do not like being confined to one area for long periods of time. On the other hand, if you like people, have an outgoing personality, and have strong communications skills, you should consider the possibility of a career in WP training or marketing support.

Exploring Career Options in Word Processing

After taking a personal inventory, you should explore career options in the field that interests you. As an aspiring WP professional, you will want to investigate all potential job options in the word processing field. Your research should result in a list of various types of WP positions, the responsibilities associated with each, skill requirements, educational requirements, working conditions, salary ranges, and opportunities for growth and advancement.

This information can be gathered from a number of different sources. There are several good WP reference sources available, in addition to this book. Appendix A provides a list of some of those reference materials. Also, you should spend some time talking to people already employed in the word processing field. Informational interviews with WP personnel can give you a much better idea of what specific jobs are really like. Finally, you may want to get in touch with professional associations, such as those listed in Appendix B. In general, such organizations can provide you with career information and may even have information about possible WP positions in your area.

Establishing Your Career Goals

Once you have taken a personal inventory and have explored possible career options, it is time to establish your personal career goals. Specifically, the kinds of questions you will want to consider include:

- What types of word processing positions interest you?
- Do you have the necessary personal traits and technical skills for those positions?
- Are you willing to return to school to develop or upgrade your skills?
- What salary do you require?
- What salary do you expect?
- In what locality do you want to find word processing employment?
- What type of company do you want to work for? Are you interested in any particular industry? Do you prefer a large or small organization?
- What kind of word processing environment do you prefer? Centralized? Decentralized? A combination of the two?
- Are you looking for full- or part-time work?
- What hours can you work?
- Are you interested in responsibility and growth potential?

The result of this process should be a clearly stated career goal. For example, your goal might be to obtain a permanent, full-time position as an entry-level word processing operator, making at least $20,000 per year, working for a publishing house in New York City. Your long-term goal might be to attain the position of

WP manager in that or a similar business within a five-year period.

BECOMING QUALIFIED

Once you have clearly outlined your WP career goals, you need to develop a strategy for achieving those goals. If you already have the educational background and skills required for the position that interests you, you can start investigating potential employers. However, if you are not yet qualified, you will need to take steps to remedy the situation.

Ask yourself the following questions: What are the minimum educational requirements and skills necessary for the position that interests me? How can I meet those requirements? (Chapter 5 describes WP training.) If you have the time and money, you should seriously consider returning to a classroom environment to obtain the necessary training. If you cannot afford full-time WP training, it is still possible to acquire WP skills. Find out whether or not your present employer offers in-house training opportunities or if the company will pay for you to attend school on a part-time basis. In addition, investigate financial aid opportunities at schools that you are interested in attending. Today, most schools offer financial assistance in the form of scholarships, grants, and loans. Information can be obtained directly from the schools' financial aid offices.

Finally, while training for a word processing career, try to get as much hands-on work experience, paid or volunteer, as you can. Experience will sharpen your skills and will make you more marketable when you enter the WP job market.

INVESTIGATING PROSPECTIVE EMPLOYERS

Because they are anxious to put their newly acquired skills to work, many people take the first job that they are offered. Do not fall into this trap. Keep in mind that finding the right employer will probably involve considerable time and research. Therefore, do not be easily discouraged; your commitment of time and energy will undoubtedly pay off in a rewarding word processing position.

Where should you look for prospective employers? The following list represents some of the more common sources of word processing employment. If possible, explore them all. In addition, be creative; use your imagination, and the right position will eventually materialize.

Your Present Company. Do you enjoy working for your present employer? If so, investigate word processing employment opportunities right in your own office. Find out about company-sponsored training programs. Many companies have their own in-house WP training programs or pay for employees to be trained outside of the company. If opportunities do exist, make sure that you let the right people know that you are interested and want to be considered. In addition, discuss opportunities for growth and advancement. There may be no need for you to extend your job search any further than your present place of employment.

School Placement Offices. Some employers list available job openings with school placement offices. They do so because of the excellent reputations associated with the graduates of particular schools. If you are currently enrolled at a school that offers WP training and they have a placement office, be sure to take advantage of this excellent job source.

Help-Wanted Advertisements. One of the easiest ways to find out about WP opportunities in your community is to read the daily and Sunday classified sections of the local newspaper. Many word processing job opportunities are listed through them. The ads can be a valuable source of information about which companies are hiring, what positions are available, the nature of particular jobs, types of equipment skills in demand, experience requirements, and salary levels.

WP help-wanted ads are also placed in magazines and newspapers associated with particular industries. If, for example, you are interested in a WP position in the advertising field, you should take a look at advertising trade journals.

Employment Services. The main goal of employment agencies and temporary help services is to match employers with employees. Employment agencies fill permanent positions while temporary services fill temporary job openings. Both types of employment services fill word-processing positions for employers, and should not be overlooked as a job source. In fact, a growing number of services specialize in word-processing job placement. These services have developed working relationships with a number of local companies and fill many of their WP positions. If you do become involved with an employment service, make sure that you understand any fee arrangements before you sign a contract.

Your Public Library. Your local public library can provide a wealth of information about prospective employers in your community and throughout the country. Business and other directories offer detailed information about a wide variety of companies and industries. Most libraries can also provide you with lists of business and professional organizations, trade associations, and community organizations that are relevant to your field of interest. The reference librarian can assist you in gathering this information.

Government Employment Offices. Federal, state, and local government organizations are major employers of WP personnel. Government employment offices or job information centers maintain lists of all currently available positions and the specific requirements for those positions. In most instances, there are standard procedures for applying for these jobs and deadlines for filing applications. You can obtain this information directly from the employment offices.

Word of Mouth. Use of personal contacts has been found to be one of the most effective ways of finding out about job openings and getting a foot in the door. Therefore, you should let as many people as possible know that you are looking for a job and describe your interests. This means family, friends, former employers, and anyone else who may have information about job openings in the word processing field.

The Phone Book. Your phone book can serve as a business directory. If you are interested in working for a particular type of business or industry, it makes sense to look in the yellow pages of your phone book for a listing of all companies in your area in that line of work.

Gathering details about prospective employers is no easy task. If possible, the information that you amass about each one should include the following: a company profile, types of WP positions available, position descriptions, necessary qualifications, salaries and other benefits, WP systems used, opportunities for advancement, and working conditions. With all of this information at your fingertips, you can then make an intelligent decision about which employers you are interested in pursuing.

PREPARING A RESUME AND COVER LETTER

In many cases, your first contact with a prospective employer will be by mail. It is important, therefore, that you prepare a cover letter and resume that will make a favorable first impression and get you an interview.

The cover letter that accompanies your resume serves a number of important functions. It briefly introduces you to the prospective employer, it expresses your interest in a particular position, it mentions your qualifications for the job, and it explains why you want to work for that particular company. Your cover letter should be brief, but interesting and informative, and, like your resume, it should be meticulously typewritten.

The resume itself should be an accurate, interesting, and attractive presentation of your background, skills, and abilities. There are many different theories as to how a resume should be organized and the types of information it should include. Certainly, you will want to put your name, address, and phone number at the very top. For a word processing position, you will need to list all word processing training and other relevant education. Also, you will need to point out all relevant work experience—paid or volunteer. You may also want to include type of work sought, honors and offices, memberships in professional associations, and references. (Most resumes end with "references available upon request.")

If you are just entering the word processing job market, you will want to stress your relevant training and educational background. If you are already employed in the WP field, emphasize both your experience and training.

The way that all this information is organized is largely a matter of personal taste and preference. There are two basic resume styles. The chronological resume lists your work experience in chronological order, beginning with your most recent job. The functional resume expresses your qualifications in categories, such as sales and management skills. It emphasizes job functions instead of dates of employment. Numerous books have been written on the resume writing process, and you should refer to several of them before making a final determination.

In some instances, you will have to go directly to a company's employment office and fill out one of their standard applications before being considered for a position. If this is the case, be sure to bring all relevant information with you, including names and phone numbers of references, and any other important names and dates. When filling out the application, be neat and thorough. It, like your resume, is a reflection of you.

INTERVIEWING

The job interview is the next step in the job-hunting process. This is often the step that terrifies interviewees and can make or break the job offer. The best way to overcome your fears is to be prepared for the interview and to keep in mind that you have a skill that is needed by the interviewer's company.

Before you go to the interview, find out as much as possible about your prospective employer and the job for which you are applying. Make a list of any questions you have, and do try to have some. If you do not know the salary being offered for the position, have a particular salary range in mind. Review your background and qualifications, and be prepared to discuss them in detail. In addition, as recommended by the U.S. Department of Labor:

- Dress appropriately.
- Show interest and enthusiasm for the job and the company. A good attitude is often as important as your actual qualifications.
- Prepare ahead of time for difficult questions. These might include: Tell me about yourself? Where do you want to be 5 or 10 years from now? What are your major strengths/weaknesses? What special contribution can you make to our organization? What kind of salary are you looking for? Why are you interested in a word processing position? How long do you plan to work for our organization?

Many career planning books offer valuable advice about the interviewing process, including how to handle such tough questions. You would be wise to spend some time reading and preparing for the job interview.

AFTER THE INTERVIEW

After every interview, be sure to thank the interviewer for his or her time, and remember to send a follow-up thank you letter. A short note of thanks often makes a lasting and favorable impression, and provides you with one more chance to express your interest in the job.

CHOOSING THE RIGHT JOB

Hopefully, the result of all of this hard work will be one or several job offers from companies that are of interest to you. In the final analysis, only you can decide which job offer is right for you. Before you make a decision, be sure to review all the facts about each position, and review your personal goals. If you are lucky, the choice will be clear!

CONTINUING TO PLAN YOUR CAREER

The fact that you are reading this book indicates your interest in planning for your future. It is important to keep in mind that career planning does not end once you find suitable employment. Indeed, it is a process that should continue throughout your professional life.

As a word-processing professional, there are a number of things that you should continue to do throughout your career. Read, take additional courses, attend trade shows and seminars, join professional associations, and develop and maintain professional contacts. By doing so, you will be helping to ensure yourself a satisfying and rewarding future in the word processing and office automation fields.

BIBLIOGRAPHY

Ahrens, Kristine A. "Word Processing: 50 Years in Retrospect." *The Office,* June 1982, 101–104.

Aschner, Katherine. *The Word Processing Handbook: A Step-by-Step Guide to Automating Your Office.* New York: Knowledge Industry Publications, 1983.

Baer, Lawrence A. and Robert J. Berkow. "Word Processing Making Headway in Law Firms." *The Office,* September 1982, 50.

Bergerud, Marly and Jean Gonzalez. *Word Processing: Concepts and Careers.* New York: John Wiley and Sons, 1981.

Boyce, Betty L. *Word Processing Concepts.* New York: McGraw-Hill, Inc., 1985.

Carron, L. Peter, Jr. *Computers: How to Break into the Field.* Cockeysville, MD: Liberty Publishing Company, 1982.

Chirlian, Barbara. *A Tenderfoot's Guide to Word Processing.* Beaverton, OR: Dilithium Press, 1982.

Cornelius, Hal and William Lewis. *Career Guide for Word Processing.* New York: Monarch Press, 1983.

Dudley, Art. *Word Processing Basics*. Englewood Cliffs, NJ: Prentice Hall, 1985.

Ellis, Bettie Hampton. *Word Processing Concepts*. New York: McGraw-Hill, Inc., 1980.

Ettinger, Blanche and Estelle Popham. *Opportunities in Office Occupations*. Chicago, IL: National Textbook Company, 1989.

Fields, Joyce S. "Word Processing: Teach Concept, Not Operation." *The Office*, June 1982, 32–34.

Flores, Ivan. *Word Processing Handbook*. New York: Van Nostrand Reinhold Company, 1983.

Foster, Timothy R.V. and Alfred Glossbrenner. *Word Processing for Executives and Professionals*. New York: Van Nostrand Reinhold Company, 1983.

Gilbert, Diana Z. "Skill in Word Processing Means More Than Just Numbers." *The Office*, October 1982, 19–22.

Glenn, Peggy. *Word Processing Profits at Home*. Huntington Beach, CA: Aames-Allen Publishing Company, 1983.

Jackson, Effie. "Office Applications for Word Processing Management." *The Office*, March 1984, 77–78.

Joner, Jacqueline. "The Many Facets of Word Processing in the Office." *The Office*, March 1984, 64.

The Kelly Report on People in the Electronic Office. Troy, MI: Kelly Services, Inc., 1982.

Kleinschrod, Walter A. *Word Processing: Operations, Applications, and Administration*. Indianapolis: The Bobbs-Merrill Company, 1980.

Konkel, Gilbert J. and Phyllis J. Peck. *Your Future in Word Processing.* New York: Richard Rosen Press, 1983.

MacMillan, Karen K. "How to Determine a Good Word Processing Operator." *The Office,* March 1983, 58.

Naclerio, Nicholas J. and Shirley A. Waterhouse. "Human Factors Can Help or Hinder Office Automation." *The Office,* September 1983, 154–156.

Noerper, Norman. *Opportunities in Data Processing Careers.* Chicago, IL: National Textbook Company, 1984.

Popyk, Marilyn K. *Word Processing: Essential Concepts.* New York: McGraw-Hill, Inc., 1983.

Prouty, Jack. *From Word Processors to Workstations.* New York: American Management Associates, 1983.

Riechers, Maggie. "Just a Secretary?" *Women's Work,* January/February 1980, 16–23.

Stultz, Russell Allen. *The Word Processing Handbook.* Englewood Cliffs, NJ: Prentice Hall, 1982.

Waite, Mitchell and Julie Arca. *Word Processing Primer.* New Hampshire: BYTE/McGraw-Hill, Inc., 1982.

Winkler, Connie. *The Computer Careers Handbook.* New York: Arco Publishing, 1983.

Witbeck, Glenda M. "Relentless Yet Rewarding: The Job of Supervising WP." *The Office,* February 1983, 67–68.

Wright, John W. and Edward J. Dwyer. *The American Almanac of Jobs and Salaries.* New York: Avon Books, 1990.

PROFESSIONAL ORGANIZATIONS

Professional organizations offer support to individuals actively involved in the word processing field. One of these organizations has graciously provided information about its objectives, scope of services, and membership requirements. Additional information can be obtained by contacting the organization directly at the address listed below.

Professional Secretaries International
   301 East Armour Boulevard
   Kansas City, Missouri 64111

PROFESSIONAL SECRETARIES INTERNATIONAL

Professional Secretaries International (PSI), headquartered in Kansas City, Missouri, is the "voice of the secretarial profession." PSI exists to promote competence and recognition of the secretarial profession and to represent the interests of those working in or preparing for secretarial and other related positions.

PSI lists among its goals and activities the following:

- To provide educational resources and opportunities for secretaries and persons in related positions to achieve and maintain the highest possible level of competence and professional development.
- To promote and provide programs for certification of professional secretaries.
- To promote a professional and cooperative relationship between the secretarial profession and employers.
- To monitor economic, governmental, and social trends that affect the secretarial profession.
- To represent the interests of the secretarial profession to media, government, business and industry, and the educational community.
- To serve as a resource and information clearinghouse on the secretarial profession.

PSI members have access to a large pool of data on the secretarial profession. PSI publishes *The Secretary Magazine* nine times per year. In addition, members receive the Code of Ethics for the Professional Secretary. Members also have access to self-study courses, can apply for PSI member loans and group insurance, and can apply for a "Certified Professional Secretary" rating. These are just some of the many benefits of a PSI membership.

GLOSSARY OF
WORD PROCESSING TERMS

Blind Word Processing System—A word processing system that does not have a video display screen.

Block Movement—A WP feature that makes it possible for a WP operator to define a block of text by marking its beginning and end with the cursor, and then to manipulate the entire block at once. For example, using this feature, a block of text can be moved to a new location in the text, deleted, or duplicated.

Boilerplate Data—Key paragraphs and phrases that are used over and over again in one or several documents.

Centering, Automatic—A WP feature that makes it possible to center a word, line, page, or even an entire document automatically.

Central Processing Unit (CPU)—The internal part of the WP equipment that is responsible for processing, storing, and retrieving data from memory. It is often called the microprocessor, or computer's brain.

Centralized Word Processing—A word processing organizational structure that involves concentrating WP equipment in a central location that services multiple departments or groups within the organization.

Command Keys—Special keys on the WP keyboard that enable the WP operator to give the machine instructions, such as delete, insert, move text, store, search, and print.

Cursor—A small character of light that shows where the next character typed by the operator will appear on the video display screen. As the operator types text into the word processor, the cursor moves across the screen to help the operator keep his or her place on the VDT.

Decentralized Word Processing—A word processing organizational structure in which smaller clusters of word processing equipment take the place of large, centralized WP pools.

Delete—A WP feature that allows you to delete, or erase, characters, words, phrases, paragraphs, or even larger blocks of text.

Display Word Processing System—A word processing system that is equipped with a video display screen.

Distributed Logic System—A category of word processing equipment in which several WP terminals share computer power, storage, and printers, and can communicate with one another. Individual terminals have some intelligence of their own.

Editing Functions—Special WP functions that make it possible for text to be keyed into the system and then revised without having to retype the entire document. Typical editing functions include insert, delete, block moves, and search.

Electronic Typewriter—A low-level word processor that contains a microprocessor, limited memory, and some additional keys that make it possible to perform basic editing and formatting functions.

Ergonomics—The application of biological and engineering data to problems pertaining to people and machines.

External Storage Devices—Mechanisms that permanently record and store information keyed into the word processing system. Typical external storage devices include magnetic disks, magnetic cards, magnetic tape, and paper tape.

File—A set of related information that is stored as a unit on an external storage device.

Formatting Functions—Special WP functions that make it possible to alter the physical appearance of a document, including width of margins, line length, and page length.

Global Search and Replace—A WP feature that makes it possible to search for a word, phrase, or sentence in a document and replace it with another.

Hard Copy—Readable copy printed on paper, as opposed to information still stored in the computer and displayed on a VDT.

Headings and Footings—Repetitive words or phrases that appear at the top and/or bottom of each printed page of a document. The automatic heading/footing feature makes it possible to type the repetitive words only once and then have the word processor print them on each page.

Hyphenation—A WP feature that makes it possible to automatically hyphenate, or break, a word that is too long to fit at the end of a line.

Impact Printer—A printer that transfers characters to paper by having an object strike an inked ribbon. Daisywheel and dot-matrix printers fall into this category.

Insert—A WP feature that allows a WP operator to add characters, words, phrases, paragraphs, and even larger blocks of text in between other words or text.

Justification—A WP feature that perfectly aligns right and left margins. In order to justify the right margin, the word processor inserts spaces of various lengths between words on each line, so that all lines appear to be the same length.

Keyboard—The device used to enter data into the word processing system. It is similar in appearance to a standard typewriter keyboard. However, the WP keyboard has some additional keys, called control keys, that can be found above or alongside the standard typing keys.

Nonimpact Printer—A printer that transfers characters to paper without striking an object against an inked ribbon. Instead, characters may be formed by such methods as heat or ink jet (spraying ink onto paper).

Office Automation—The use of computers in office equipment to streamline operations.

Operators—Those individuals who run the WP equipment. They are responsible for typing, or keying, data into the word processor.

Principals—Those individuals who originate documents for input into the WP system. They are also referred to as authors or document originators.

Printer—The device that produces hard copies of your text. Unlike the standard typewriter, the WP printer is generally used only after the document is completed, not throughout the production process.

Random Access Memory (RAM)—WP memory that temporarily stores and handles all information given to the word processor, and can later be erased.

Read Only Memory (ROM)—The WP system's permanent memory. It stores the machine's operating instructions which tell the CPU how to perform various functions.

Scrolling—A WP feature that makes possible the upward/downward or left/right movement of text lines so that additional text can be seen on the video display screen.

Search—The ability of the WP system to look for a word or group of words that appear in text and to display them on the VDT.

Shared Logic Systems—A category of WP equipment in which several WP terminals share the storage and processing power of one central computer. Unlike stand-alone or distributed logic systems, shared logic terminals are essentially ''dumb''—they cannot function without the aid of another computer.

Soft Copy—Text stored in a computer and visible only on a VDT, rather than printed out on paper.

Spelling Verification—A WP feature that checks the spelling of the words in a document against the WP system's own internal dictionary.

Stand-Alone Word Processor—A word processor that is totally self-contained. That is, it can function on its own without the aid of another computer.

User Friendly—Easy for a user to understand and operate.

Video Display Terminal (VDT)—A device, similar to a television screen, that allows you to see a soft copy of your text as it is being typed into the WP system, but before it is actually printed out.

Word Processing—A system of personnel, procedures, and WP equipment that provides efficient and economical printed business communications.

Word Wrap—A WP feature that eliminates the need to hit the return key when you reach the end of a line. Instead, the word processor automatically jumps to the next line when you reach the right margin.

VGM CAREER BOOKS

OPPORTUNITIES IN
Available in both paperback and
hardbound editions
Accounting Careers
Acting Careers
Advertising Careers
Aerospace Careers
Agriculture Careers
Airline Careers
Animal and Pet Care
Appraising Valuation Science
Architecture
Automotive Service
Banking
Beauty Culture
Biological Sciences
Biotechnology Careers
Book Publishing Careers
Broadcasting Careers
Building Construction Trades
Business Communication Careers
Business Management
Cable Television
Carpentry Careers
Chemical Engineering
Chemistry Careers
Child Care Careers
Chiropractic Health Care
Civil Engineering Careers
Commercial Art and Graphic Design
Computer Aided Design and
 Computer Aided Mfg.
Computer Maintenance Careers
Computer Science Careers
Counseling & Development
Crafts Careers
Culinary Careers
Dance
Data Processing Careers
Dental Care
Drafting Careers
Electrical Trades
Electronic and Electrical Engineering
Energy Careers
Engineering Careers
Engineering Technology Careers
Environmental Careers
Eye Care Careers
Fashion Careers
Fast Food Careers
Federal Government Careers
Film Careers
Financial Careers
Fire Protection Services
Fitness Careers
Food Services
Foreign Language Careers
Forestry Careers
Gerontology Careers
Government Service
Graphic Communications
Health and Medical Careers
High Tech Careers
Home Economics Careers
Hospital Administration
Hotel & Motel Management
Human Resources Management
 Careers

Industrial Design
Information Systems Careers
Insurance Careers
Interior Design
International Business
Journalism Careers
Landscape Architecture
Laser Technology
Law Careers
Law Enforcement and Criminal Justice
Library and Information Science
Machine Trades
Magazine Publishing Careers
Management
Marine & Maritime Careers
Marketing Careers
Materials Science
Mechanical Engineering
Medical Technology Careers
Microelectronics
Military Careers
Modeling Careers
Music Careers
Newspaper Publishing Careers
Nursing Careers
Nutrition Careers
Occupational Therapy Careers
Office Occupations
Opticianry
Optometry
Packaging Science
Paralegal Careers
Paramedical Careers
Part-time & Summer Jobs
Performing Arts Careers
Petroleum Careers
Pharmacy Careers
Photography
Physical Therapy Careers
Physician Careers
Plumbing & Pipe Fitting
Podiatric Medicine
Printing Careers
Property Management Careers
Psychiatry
Psychology
Public Health Careers
Public Relations Careers
Purchasing Careers
Real Estate
Recreation and Leisure
Refrigeration and Air Conditioning
 Trades
Religious Service
Restaurant Careers
Retailing
Robotics Careers
Sales Careers
Sales & Marketing
Secretarial Careers
Securities Industry
Social Science Careers
Social Work Careers
Speech-Language Pathology Careers
Sports & Athletics
Sports Medicine
State and Local Government
Teaching Careers

Technical Communications
Telecommunications
Television and Video Careers
Theatrical Design & Production
Transportation Careers
Travel Careers
Veterinary Medicine Careers
Vocational and Technical Careers
Welding Careers
Word Processing
Writing Careers
Your Own Service Business

CAREERS IN
Accounting
Advertising
Business
Communications
Computers
Education
Engineering
Health Care
Science

CAREER DIRECTORIES
Careers Encyclopedia
Occupational Outlook Handbook

CAREER PLANNING
Admissions Guide to Selective
 Business Schools
Career Planning and Development for
 College Students and Recent
 Graduates
Careers Checklists
Careers for Bookworms and
 Other Literary Types
Careers for Sports Nuts
Handbook of Business and
 Management Careers
Handbook of Scientific and
 Technical Careers
How to Change Your Career
How to Get and Get Ahead
 On Your First Job
How to Get People to Do Things
 Your Way
How to Have a Winning Job Interview
How to Land a Better Job
How to Make the Right Career Moves
How to Prepare for College
How to Run Your Own Home Business
How to Write a Winning Résumé
Joyce Lain Kennedy's Career Book
Life Plan
Planning Your Career of Tomorrow
Planning Your College Education
Planning Your Military Career
Planning Your Young Child's
 Education

SURVIVAL GUIDES
Dropping Out or Hanging In
High School Survival Guide
College Survival Guide

VGM Career Horizons
a division of *NTC Publishing Group*
4255 West Touhy Avenue
Lincolnwood, Illinois 60646-1975